# COUPLES DEVOTIONAL

A DEVOTIONAL THAT ENHANCES
COMMUNICATION, DEEPENS FAITH,
SIMPLIFIES SCRIPTURE, FOSTERS INTIMACY,
AND PROVIDES CONFLICT RESOLUTION
TOOLS, HELPING COUPLES BUILD A STRONG,
CHRIST-CENTERED RELATIONSHIP

## REVEREND FRED D. REESE

# CONTENTS

# INTRODUCTION

One evening, I sat with a couple in my office. They were clutching their Bibles, eyes full of hope and a little bit of fear. They had hit a rough patch, like we all do sometimes. He felt unheard, and she felt unloved. They were stuck in a cycle of miscommunication that many couples know all too well. As we talked, I saw a spark reignite when they realized they were not alone. They began to see their faith as a guide to understanding and healing. Their story is one of many that shows the incredible power of a Christ-centered relationship.

This book is here to help you find that same power. It aims to strengthen your relationship through better communication, a deeper faith, and practical conflict resolution tools. We'll simplify scripture so it speaks directly to the heart of your relationship. The goal is to build a strong, loving, and resilient bond centered on Christ.

Let me introduce myself. I am Rev. Fred Reese, a Baptist minister with over 20 years of experience leading couples' ministries. I'm blessed to be married to Geraldine for 46 years and counting. God has been good to us. My passion is helping couples strengthen their marriages. I've seen firsthand how biblical guidance can transform relationships. How can I say that? Geri and I submitted to a similar biblical guidance, which made a massive difference. It's a privilege to share this journey with you.

Here's a roadmap of what you'll find in this book. We'll start with the book of Genesis, in which God placed Adam in the Garden of Eden. Every couple must come to an understanding of God's intentions for Adam and, later, Eve. It's in the Garden of Eden where today's couple can gain knowledge of their roles and responsibilities as they enter the marriage bond. Next, we will visit communication skills. You'll learn to talk and listen to each other with love and respect. Next, we'll integrate faith into your daily lives, helping you grow spiritually as a couple. We'll also explore intimacy and how to nurture it in a Christ-centered way. Each chapter builds on the last, providing a comprehensive toolkit for a thriving relationship.

This book offers unique features that set it apart from other devotionals. It provides actionable exercises to try together, real-life success stories to inspire you, and various content covering different aspects of relationships. It's not just about reading; it's about doing, learning, and growing together.

Many of you want to deepen your spiritual journey and strengthen your relationship. You might be feeling the stress of daily life, struggling to find time for each other, or seeking ways to connect on a deeper level. This book speaks to those needs. It's designed for adults aged 30-50, but anyone seeking to enrich their relationship will find value here.

I invite you to participate actively in this journey. Take the lessons and exercises to heart, apply them to your relationships, and share your experiences. This is not just a book to read; it's a guide to living a Christ-centered relationship.

As you turn the pages, be prepared for a transformative journey. Together, we'll build a loving, resilient, and Christ-centered relationship. You'll find joy and strength in each other and your faith. This book is your companion on that journey, and I'm honored to walk it with you.

So, please grab a cup of coffee, cozy up with your spouse, and embark on this adventure together. I'm excited to see where this journey takes you.

# CHAPTER 1
# LAYING THE FOUNDATION

Have you ever wondered why some couples seem to glide through life together, hand in hand, while others struggle to make it to the following day without a fight? It's like watching a perfectly choreographed dance versus two left feet tripping over one another. The secret to that graceful dance can often be traced to having a strong foundation. Like a house built on rock rather than sand, a marriage rooted in faith and understanding can withstand the storms of life. This chapter is about setting up that solid foundation, and we'll start with the oldest couple in the book—literally. No, not the couple next door with the vintage vinyl collection, but Adam and Eve, the first pair to give marriage a go. Their story provides a blueprint for marriage, showing us what works and what doesn't and how God's intentions for companionship and unity can guide us even today.

## 1.1 GOD'S BLUEPRINT FOR MARRIAGE: UNDERSTANDING ADAM AND EVE

Let's look at the creation story, a tale as old as time. God created Adam and Eve in the garden, not as an afterthought but as a spouse. This wasn't just about having someone to split the chores with; it was about companionship and marriage. God saw that it wasn't good for Adam to be alone, so He created Eve as a helper and equal. Eve's role was to help Adam accomplish the tasks God would assign. Their instructions were to multiply, be fruitful, subdue, and have dominion over everything in the garden. In this divine marriage, Adam and Eve were meant to support each other, reflecting God's intention of unity and mutual support. This team effort is a reminder that marriage is about walking side by side, not one leading the other. It's important to understand that being the help meet is an honor as God is asking you to help man accomplish those tasks God has for man. It is not a subservient role. Worldly understanding and application contribute to why today's wives do not fully embrace the helper role.

The Garden of Eden also teaches us some hard lessons. The fall of Adam and Eve is a cautionary tale about the consequences of straying from God's path. Marriage involves vulnerability and transparency—two things they had in spades before the infamous fruit incident. Their story shows us that cracks form in the foundation when you hide or blame, as Adam did. But here's the silver lining: it also highlights the importance of joint stewardship and responsibility. They were entrusted with the garden, just as couples nurture their relationship. Failure occurs because of non-compliance. The fall reminds us that both spouses have roles to play, and shirking these duties can lead to dissatisfaction.

Genesis 2:24: *"Now therefore a man shall leave his father and mother and share cleave unto his wife and they shall be one flesh."* The concept of becoming 'one flesh' is the ultimate goal in marriage. The two individuals come from different lifestyles and have different opinions and mindsets. And yet, with God's help, the couple can achieve oneness in their marriage. This is more than poetic language; it's a profound theological idea. In marriage, two individuals become one, both in body, spirit, and purpose. It's a union that calls for commitment to shared life and goals. This oneness means making decisions together, facing challenges as a team, and supporting each other's dreams. Just as God intended Adam and Eve to navigate life as a single unit, modern couples are encouraged to blend their hopes, dreams, and lives into one cohesive entity. This union is sacred, blending beyond the every day to touch the eternal. It's the hardest for a couple to embrace, but it is the most rewarding time for the couple as they realize with God, *"all things are possible."*

A marriage without God is like a ship without a compass. Reflecting on the role of God in marriage, it's clear that His presence is not just beneficial; it's vital. Please remember: It was God's idea from the beginning. Prayer and spiritual guidance are the north star, providing direction during turbulent times. Faith is the anchor, holding the ship steady when the seas get rough. Couples who pray together tap into a well of strength, finding peace and clarity in God's wisdom. Faith becomes the lens through which challenges are viewed, turning obstacles into opportunities for growth. With God at the center, marriages are not just surviving—they are thriving, embodying the love and unity that Adam and Eve were first called to reflect. Fact: *"A threefold cord is not quickly broken."* *(Ecclesiastes 4:12).*

## 1.2 EMBRACING OUR CALLING: ROLES AND RESPONSIBILITIES IN MARRIAGE

Understanding responsibilities within marriage can feel like trying to assemble furniture without instructions—every part is essential, but it's easy to get confused. The good news is that the Bible provides a blueprint, though it's more flexible than rigid. Mutual submission and love are the cornerstones. Picture it as a dance where spouses lead and follow, stepping in time with each other.

Ephesians 5:21-33 speaks to this mutual submission, urging us to put our spouse's needs before our own. Verse #22, *"Wives, submit yourselves unto your husbands, as unto the Lord."* As the helpmeet, Wife, God asks you to submit to your husband. Your submission is not about the man but your willingness to trust God. Verse #25, "Husbands, God is asking you "to love your wife. That love is comparable to Christ loving the church." That's a sacrificial type of love. Here's the picture: with God in the marriage, the wife learns to submit while the husband is asked to love the wife, similarly to how Christ loved the church. The wife is not in a servant role. The idea of the submission accomplishes two things: It allows the wife to yield in the decision process, thus yielding decision-making to the husband, who has been tasked to lead as Christ was the head of the church. Men, you must commit to your responsibilities and lead your family as God designated. Men, you are not a Boss. You are tasked to be the godly example for your family and lead them in a way pleasing God. Execution of both roles and responsibilities is about how we support and uplift each other, ensuring that both voices are heard and valued.

Marriage thrives on functioning as a team. It's not just about splitting chores, though that's important too. It's about making decisions together and solving problems as a team. Imagine running a household like a small business where everyone has roles but shares the same mission. You might be the CEO of the kitchen, while your spouse is the CFO of finances, but both of you are equally invested in the enterprise's success. This collaborative spirit turns challenges into opportunities for growth, ensuring that both spouses are pulling in the same direction.

We can interpret these biblical roles with modern sensibilities in today's world. Flexibility and adaptability are key. Roles are no longer strictly defined by traditional gender lines. Instead, they're shaped by individual strengths and preferences. It's crucial to keep the lines of communication open and regularly discuss expectations and needs. Maybe one spouse loves cooking, while the other prefers organizing. Embrace these differences and use them to craft a balanced and fulfilling marriage that works uniquely for you.

In real life, these roles manifest in a myriad of ways. Consider a couple who makes it a point to pray together every morning. This shared spiritual practice sets the tone for their day, aligning their goals and reinforcing their marriage. They might also tackle household duties together, transforming mundane tasks into opportunities for connection. Balancing career and family responsibilities requires teamwork. Perhaps one spouse takes on more at home while the other focuses on a career, or they might juggle work and family, supporting each other through the chaos. Communication, compromise, and a shared commitment to what matters most are the key. Abandoning or refusing to embrace one's role/responsibilities will present a negative result as the sponsor will not adhere to their role or responsibilities. Properly executed, it creates a harmonious 360 connection where the man is leading and loving while the wife is helping and allowing the husband to lead. This might surprise you, but it is a fact: Wives do not want to lead. They want their husbands to lead and love as God has designed.

***Exercise: Reflect on Your Roles Together***

Take some time to discuss your roles and responsibilities. Ask each other: What tasks do I enjoy, and which ones do I find draining? How can we support each other better? Use this opportunity to align your roles with your strengths and preferences, fostering a more harmonious marriage. Learning and executing your role and responsibilities will take patience and time. Final thought: men's passivity is a sin. God is asking for your leadership. Failure will ultimately hurt the relationship.

## 1.3 BUILDING ON THE ROCK: ANCHORING YOUR RELATIONSHIP IN FAITH

Imagine your marriage as a beautiful, sturdy house. You wouldn't build it on shifting sands, would you? You'd want a solid, unshakeable foundation. Faith plays a similar role in marriage. It's the bedrock that keeps everything steady. The reliability of scripture acts like a blueprint for married life, offering guidance on everything from love and patience to forgiveness and grace. Think of it as your go-to manual when life throws you a curveball. Regular worship and spiritual practices are like the daily maintenance that keeps this foundation strong. They help you reconnect with each other and God, reminding you of your union's larger picture and purpose. Getting caught up in the hustle and bustle of daily life is easy, but carving out time for spiritual activities ensures that your relationship remains rooted and grounded.

Regarding faith-building activities, attending church services together is an excellent starting point. It's like a weekly tune-up for your soul, offering a shared space to reflect and recharge. Equally important are couple's Bible studies, which allow you to delve deeper into scripture and discuss its relevance to your lives. These sessions can spark insightful conversations and lead to shared revelations, helping you grow individually and as a couple. And let's not forget about shared prayer and reflection. Taking a few moments each day to pray together can work wonders for your relationship. It's an intimate act that fosters emotional closeness, reinforcing that you're in this together, come what may.

Hebrews 12:11 defines faith *"as the substance of things hoped for and the evidence of things not seen."* Faith acts as a powerful adhesive, binding you together in times of trial. A strong faith base equips you with enhanced resilience, enabling you to face life's inevitable challenges with grace and confidence. When the winds of adversity blow, as they sometimes do, faith is an anchor, keeping you from drifting apart. It deepens your emotional and spiritual connection, creating a profound and enduring bond. Couples who make faith a central part of their relationship often find they are better equipped to handle stress, communicate effectively, and support one another through thick and thin. It's like having an extra layer of armor that shields and protects your union.

Take, for instance, the story of a couple I once worked with. They faced a significant crisis when one spouse lost their job. It was stressful and uncertain, but they turned to their faith instead of letting it drive a wedge between them. They prayed together, asking for guidance and strength. They sought wisdom from scripture, finding reassurance in passages about God's provision and care. Their faith saw them through the crisis and deepened their relationship, reinforcing their commitment to each other. This is just one of many examples of how faith can sustain and uplift a marriage.

In another case, a couple set a faith-driven goal to serve in their community. They volunteered regularly, bringing meals to those in need. This shared endeavor strengthened their bond and gave them a sense of purpose and fulfillment. It was a tangible expression of their faith and a way to live out their values. These stories illustrate the transformative power of faith, showing how it can turn challenges into opportunities for growth and connection.

So, whether you're praying together, attending church, or simply reflecting on scripture, know that you are building something lasting and meaningful. Your marriage, grounded in faith, is a testament to the strength and beauty of anchoring your lives on the rock of divine love and guidance.

## 1.4 THE POWER OF COMMITMENT: COVENANT RELATIONSHIPS

Picture marriage as a dance, not where you nervously sway at a high school dance, but a grand waltz with sweeping movements and an innate rhythm. At the heart of this dance is a covenant relationship—a concept that might seem a bit archaic but sticks with me. Unlike a contract, which is all about terms and conditions, a covenant is sacred and permanent, akin to promising your favorite dessert for life without a calorie count. It's a commitment that reaches deep, intertwining spiritual beliefs with emotional depth. A covenant isn't just about two people; it's about two people and God. It's a promise made in the heart, witnessed by heaven, and carried out with devotion.

What does this look like in daily life, you ask? Consider a covenant a warm, cozy blanket of unconditional love and forgiveness. It means when your spouse eats the last cookie, you don't hold it against them for eternity. Instead, you laugh, forgive, and maybe bake another batch together. Perseverance and dedication are the threads that weave this blanket together. In a covenant relationship, love doesn't waver with the seasons; it holds firm, even when life throws curveballs. It's about sticking it out, not because you have to, but because you choose to every day. This commitment transforms how you handle disagreements, approach challenges, and celebrate victories. The steadfast heart of the relationship beats with a rhythm of unity and strength.

The Bible offers rich examples of covenants that can guide us. The covenant between God and His people is a beautiful, unwavering commitment and love model. God's promises, like those to Abraham, are steadfast and enduring, not contingent on perfect behavior. These biblical examples remind us that a faithful covenant doesn't back down when things get tough. Instead, it leans in, drawing strength from promises and love that transcend time. Scripture contains stories and teachings illuminating what living out a covenant relationship means. These stories become a compass, guiding couples through the trials and triumphs of life.

### Creating a Covenant: Crafting Your Marriage Mission Statement

Let's discuss practical ways to embody these covenant principles in your relationship. One way is by creating a marriage mission statement. This isn't a corporate memo but a heartfelt declaration of your shared values and goals. It can be as simple or detailed as you like, capturing what matters most. Maybe it includes a commitment to kindness, adventure, or raising a family rooted in faith. Another way to embody covenant principles is by regularly renewing your vows or commitments. It doesn't have to be a grand ceremony; it could be a quiet moment over coffee where you look each other in the eyes and reaffirm your promises. These practices remind you of the depth and beauty of your covenant, helping keep it vibrant and alive. By integrating these elements into your lives, you create a relationship that's not only enduring but also profoundly fulfilling.

### Creating a Shared Vision: Aligning Relationship Goals

Imagine marriage as a road trip. You've got your destination in mind, snacks packed, and playlists ready. But what happens if your GPS starts glitching, and suddenly, one of you is set on heading to the beach while the other insists on the mountains? Frustrating, right? That's where the magic of shared goals comes in. Having a unified vision is like having a trusty map that guides your journey together. It ensures you're steering the wheel in the same direction, aligning on core values and life plans. This alignment is crucial because it strengthens your bonds, creating a cohesive unit that moves through life with purpose and direction. Shared dreams aren't just about big-picture aspirations; they're about the little things, too—like deciding where to live or how to spend a weekend. They provide a framework that keeps your relationship grounded and focused on what truly matters.

Now, let's talk about setting those goals. It might sound like a daunting task, akin to assembling IKEA furniture without instructions, but it's simpler than you think. Start with regular discussions about where you both see yourselves in the short and long term. These conversations can happen over dinner or during a relaxed weekend stroll. The key is to keep the dialogue open and honest, allowing each spouse to express their hopes and concerns. Once you've got your ideas, it's time to set realistic, faith-aligned goals. These should reflect your shared values and aspirations, serving as stepping stones toward your larger vision. Establish accountability measures, too. This doesn't mean policing each other but supporting and encouraging one another, celebrating progress, and adjusting plans as needed.

The impact of shared goals on your relationship is profound. They foster increased cooperation and teamwork, turning you into a dynamic duo ready to tackle whatever life throws at you. With a clear sense of purpose and direction, you'll find that everyday challenges become more manageable. Instead of feeling like you're pulling in different directions, you'll move forward together, hand in hand. This alignment strengthens your bond and enhances your relationship's resilience, allowing you to weather storms confidently and gracefully.

To make this process easier, consider creating a vision board. Think of it as a visual representation of your shared dreams and goals. Gather images, quotes, and symbols that resonate with both of you and arrange them on a board. This can be a fun and creative way to visualize your future, constantly reminding you of what you're working towards. You might also use templates for goal-setting discussions, providing a structured planning and reflection format. These tools can guide your conversations, helping you stay focused and organized.

As you set out on this path, remember that the journey is as important as the destination. Enjoy the process of dreaming and planning together. Revel in the shared sense of accomplishment as you hit milestones and adapt to changes. By aligning your vision and working towards common goals, you're building a future together and weaving a rich tapestry of experiences, memories, and love that will continue to grow and evolve, strengthening your relationship in ways you never imagined. So dream big, plan thoughtfully, and cherish each step.

# CHAPTER 2
## ENHANCING COMMUNICATION

Picture this: you're at a fancy restaurant, candles flickering, the aroma of garlic bread wafting through the air. You look across the table at your spouse, and instead of discussing the day, you're locked in a silent battle of "Who's going to speak first?" Sometimes, it feels like speaking a different language altogether. And in a way, you might be. That's where the concept of love languages comes in. Dr. Gary Chapman, a marriage counselor and author, introduced this idea to help people understand that just like we have different languages spoken worldwide, there are other ways we express and receive love.

In his book, Chapman identifies five love languages: words of affirmation, acts of service, receiving gifts, quality time, and physical touch. Words of affirmation are about expressing love through verbal compliments and appreciation.

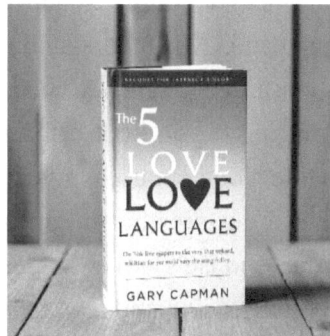

Think of it as a verbal high-five.

Acts of service involve doing things for your spouse that show you care, like cooking dinner or washing the car. Receiving gifts isn't about materialism but the thought and effort behind a present that makes someone feel cherished. Quality time requires giving someone your undivided attention, whether it's a cozy movie night or a walk in the park. Lastly, physical touch includes gestures like holding hands or a warm hug that conveys affection without words. Understanding these languages can significantly improve how you connect with your spouse.

But how do you figure out your spouse's primary love language? Simple. You could take a love language quiz together, which is a fun and insightful activity. There are quizzes online, but for time's sake, try https://5lovelanguages.com. These quizzes will help you discover how you naturally prefer to express and receive love. Alternatively, pay attention to how your spouse reacts to different expressions of love. Do they light up when you surprise them with a gift, or do they feel most appreciated when you verbally acknowledge their efforts? Observing these reactions can provide valuable clues. It's like being a love detective, only without the trench coat.

Communication can become more fulfilling once you've cracked the code on your spouse's love language. You create a bridge that enhances emotional connection and satisfaction by speaking their language. Misunderstandings and conflicts often arise when one spouse feels unloved because their love language isn't spoken. Imagine if you kept offering acts of service, like doing the dishes, while your spouse craved words of affirmation. Both are meaningful gestures but might not hit the mark if they don't align with your spouse's love language. Understanding these nuances can reduce tension and lead to more harmonious interactions.

Now, let's get into the nitty-gritty of expressing each love language with practical tips. Plan a surprise date night for quality time to focus solely on each other. It doesn't have to be extravagant—a picnic in the backyard can be just as special. If your spouse's love language is words of affirmation, try writing a heartfelt note or even leaving little sticky notes around the house with messages of love and appreciation. Regarding acts of service, preparing a favorite meal or tackling a chore they dislike can speak volumes. For those whose love language is receiving gifts, a small, thoughtful present can make them feel seen and valued. Lastly, if physical touch is their language, never underestimate the power of a spontaneous hug or holding hands during a walk.

Understanding and speaking your spouse's love language is like finding the correct key for a lock; it opens the door to deeper connection and understanding. It's about making a conscious effort to express love in a way that resonates with them. So, grab your detective hat—or not—and embark on this delightful journey of discovery. You might find that the language of love has been in your hands all along.

## 2.1 ACTIVE LISTENING: HEARING BEYOND WORDS

Imagine you're at a concert, but instead of listening to the music, you're too busy reading the program or texting a friend. You'd miss the whole point. That's what happens in conversations when we don't practice active listening. Active listening isn't just about hearing words; it's about fully engaging with your spouse. It means focusing entirely on the speaker and showing genuine interest in what they're saying. This isn't the time to plan your grocery list or think about your witty comeback. It's about being present and attentive, giving your spouse the gift of your undivided attention. When you actively listen, you convey that you care about what they're saying and that their thoughts and feelings matter to you. This is crucial for building trust and understanding in any relationship. I often suggest that couples deploy God's communications as outlined in James 1:19: *"Wherefore, my beloved brethren, let every man be swift to hear, slow to speak, and slow to wrath."*

To improve your listening skills, consider some practical techniques that make active listening a breeze. Reflective listening, for example, involves paraphrasing your spouse's words to ensure you understand correctly. It's like being a mirror, reflecting their thoughts to them. This shows that you're engaged and helps clarify any misunderstandings. Another helpful method is to avoid interruptions and focus on non-verbal cues. Sometimes, what isn't said is just as important as what is. Pay attention to body language, facial expressions, and tone of voice. These non-verbal signals often convey more than words alone. Finally, practice being fully present. Turn off the TV, close your phone, and make eye contact. Show that you're not just hearing them; you're truly listening.

However, there are common barriers that can hinder effective listening. We live in a world of distractions, from the constant ping of notifications to the lure of multitasking. It's easy to get sidetracked, but these distractions can prevent you from fully engaging in the conversation. Another barrier is prejudgment, which occurs when we make assumptions about what our spouse will say before they even say it. This can lead to misunderstandings and missed opportunities for connection. We all have biases and beliefs, but recognizing and setting them aside is essential for active listening. Doing so opens the door to truly understanding your spouse's perspective.

Try some practical exercises that implement these techniques to enhance your listening skills. One effective exercise is role-playing scenarios, where you practice reflective listening. Take turns being the speaker and the listener. After your spouse speaks, paraphrase what they've said to confirm your understanding. This sharpens your skills and deepens your connection as you learn more about each other's viewpoints. Another helpful exercise is to engage in listening sessions with timed speaking and feedback. Set a timer and let one spouse speak for a few minutes without interruption. When the time is up, the listener provides feedback or reflects on what was said. This practice helps stay focused and resist the urge to interrupt, fostering a more open and effective dialogue.

Active listening may seem simple, but its impact on relationships is profound. It transforms everyday conversations into opportunities for deeper connection and understanding. By honing these skills, you create a space where both spouses feel heard, valued, and understood. It's like tuning into a favorite radio station where every word and note resonates, creating a harmonious relationship melody. As you practice active listening, you'll find that it enhances your communication and strengthens the bond you share, making each conversation a meaningful exchange of thoughts, feelings, and love. In its simple way, Godly communication, as mentioned in the book of James, embraces active listening.

## 2.2 NAVIGATING DIFFICULT CONVERSATIONS: TOOLS FOR CONSTRUCTIVE DIALOGUE

Imagine you're about to discuss a tricky topic with your spouse. Perhaps it's about finances or parenting styles. Your heart races, your palms sweat, and suddenly, your mind is blank. It's like preparing for a challenging hike without a map. But fear not because setting the stage for these conversations is vital. First, choose a safe and neutral environment, like a cozy living room or a quiet café, where distractions are minimal and you both feel comfortable. This isn't about ambushing your spouse with heavy topics over breakfast. It's about being intentional. Next, clarify your intentions and desired outcomes. Are you looking to solve a problem or express your feelings? Clarifying what you hope to achieve lays the groundwork for a productive dialogue. Think of it as plotting your course before setting sail. Through my daughter (Von), I understood the concept of a team in marriage. Utilizing the team concept can soften conversations in difficult times. When a team realizes they are losing the game (especially one they support to win), each member reaches deep inside and does the work necessary to secure the victory. Losing is not an option.

Once the stage is set, the key is to maintain constructiveness throughout the conversation. One effective technique is using "I" statements to express your feelings and needs. For example, instead of saying, "You never help with the chores," try, "I feel overwhelmed when the housework piles up, and I need your help to manage it." This shift in language reduces defensiveness and focuses on your experience rather than blaming your spouse. It's like speaking from the heart rather than pointing a finger. Staying focused on the issue at hand is equally important. Avoid veering into personal attacks or bringing up past grievances. Keep the conversation on track by addressing the specific topic and working collaboratively toward a resolution. Imagine it as a focused dance, where spouses move in harmony rather than stepping on each other's toes.

Empathy plays a starring role in these conversations. It's about understanding your spouse's perspective and validating their feelings. Practice mirroring emotions to demonstrate understanding. If they express frustration, acknowledge it with, "I hear that you're frustrated, and I understand why." This simple act can defuse tension and create a sense of connection. Asking open-ended questions also helps. Instead of assuming you know what they're thinking, ask, "How do you feel about this?" or "What's your perspective?" These questions invite deeper insights and foster a more open dialogue. It's like exploring uncharted territory together, discovering new facets of each other's experiences. Please, don't fall into the trap of reading your spouse's mind. You can't! It only compounds the problem.

Real-life scenarios provide valuable lessons in navigating difficult conversations. Consider a couple facing financial disagreements. One spouse might prioritize saving for the future, while the other prefers enjoying the present. They could start by acknowledging each other's values and concerns to address this. "I understand why saving is important to you, but I also value making memories now." They can create a balanced financial approach by finding common ground and discussing shared goals. Similarly, addressing parenting style differences requires collaboration and flexibility. Perhaps one spouse leans toward discipline while the other emphasizes nurturing. They could explore various parenting resources and agree on strategies incorporating both approaches. It's about blending strengths and creating a unified front.

## 2.3 FROM MISUNDERSTANDING TO CLARITY: BREAKING DOWN COMMUNICATION BARRIERS

Picture this: you're having what you think is a simple conversation with your spouse about weekend plans, and suddenly, it spirals into a heated debate about who left the milk out last night. How did you get here? Often, communication barriers sneak in like uninvited guests, causing chaos in what should be a peaceful gathering. One common culprit is misinterpretation due to tone or body language. A simple "fine" can sound like an agreement or a declaration of impending doom, depending on how it's said. Add a raised eyebrow or crossed arms, and suddenly, you're navigating a minefield. These subtle cues can drastically alter the message, leading to confusion and frustration. Even cultural and background differences can act as barriers. You might see certain gestures or phrases as affectionate, while your spouse perceives them as dismissive. These differences in perception can lead to misunderstandings, making it feel like you speak different dialects of the same language.

So, how do you bridge this gap? One effective strategy is to ask clarifying questions. If you're unsure about what your spouse means, ask. "When you said you were fine, did you mean you're okay, or is there something more?" This approach shows that you're engaged and helps prevent assumptions from taking root. Another helpful technique is establishing regular check-ins. These are dedicated times to discuss ongoing issues and clear up any misunderstandings. Think of it as a relationship tune-up, ensuring everything runs smoothly and addressing potential hiccups before they become full-blown breakdowns.

Assumptions can be like those pesky weeds in a garden—they grow quickly and can choke out the beautiful flowers of understanding. We close the door to open dialogue when we assume we know what our spouse thinks. These assumptions can lead to miscommunication, causing unnecessary conflict. Encouraging open dialogue is crucial in dispelling these misunderstandings. Invite your spouse to share their thoughts and feelings without fear of judgment. It's about creating a safe space where both spouses feel comfortable expressing themselves. This openness can transform assumptions into opportunities for deeper understanding and connection.

To build and refine your communication skills, consider engaging in exercises designed to promote clarity. Practicing dialogue with feedback from a third party can be incredibly insightful. Imagine a friend or counselor acting as a referee, helping you both see where communication might go astray and offering constructive feedback. This practice can illuminate blind spots and strengthen your ability to communicate effectively. Mindfulness exercises can also improve focus during conversations. Practicing mindfulness teaches you to stay present, reduce distractions, and enhance your ability to engage fully with your spouse. It's like training your mind to focus on the conversation rather than wandering off to your to-do list or what's for dinner.

Improving communication takes effort, but the rewards are worth it. You create a foundation of trust and understanding by breaking down barriers and fostering open dialogue. Instead of navigating a minefield of misunderstandings, you find yourselves on a path of clarity and connection. It's about turning those uninvited guests into welcome allies, ensuring that every conversation brings you closer together.

## 2.4 THE ART OF APOLOGY: HEALING THROUGH FORGIVENESS

Imagine a scenario where you've just argued with your spouse. The room feels colder, and the silence is deafening. It's a situation we've all found ourselves in, and it begs the question: how do we heal and move forward? Apologizing is not just a formality; it's a bridge to restoring trust and emotional connection. When we apologize sincerely, we acknowledge the hurt caused and open the door to healing. It's like saying, "I see your pain, and I'm here to mend it." Apologies are the glue that can repair the cracks in a relationship, making it stronger and more resilient.

But what makes an apology genuine and sincere? It's not just about uttering the words "I'm sorry." A meaningful apology involves acknowledging the hurt you've caused and taking responsibility for your actions. This means saying, "I know I hurt you, and I own that." It's about offering to make amends and committing to change, showing that you are willing to put in the effort to prevent the issue from happening again. An apology should be more than words; it should be a promise to do better. Think of it as a roadmap for rebuilding trust and ensuring both spouses feel valued and respected.

Now, let's explore the role of forgiveness in this healing process. Forgiveness is a Godly principle that humanity is still learning. The lack of forgiveness is a major contributor to the divorce rate among Christian couples. Forgiveness is often misunderstood. It's not about forgetting the offense or minimizing its impact. Instead, it's about letting go of the bitterness and resentment that can fester over time. In the gospel of Matthew 6:14, Jesus tells us, *"For if ye forgive men their trespasses, your heavenly Father will also forgive you."* Later in Matthew's writing, Matthew 18:21, *"The came Peter to him (Jesus), and said Lord, how oft shall my brother sin against me, and I forgive him? Til seven times? Verse#22 Jesus said unto him (Peter) I say not unto thee, Until seven times: but, Until seventy times seven."* Of course, Jesus was talking about forgiveness up 490 times. Jesus was saying we should be willing to forgive all the time. Reasoning for all the time is each day we wake up, God forgives us through His grace and mercy. We serve a God willing to look past all our faults and meet our needs. Forgiveness is a gift you give to yourself as much as to your spouse. It allows you to move forward without being weighed down by the past. However, forgiveness requires time and patience. It's a process, not a one-time event. Some wounds take longer to heal, and that's okay. What matters is the willingness to work through them together, hand in hand.

To practice the art of apologizing and forgiving, consider starting with an exercise in writing apology letters. Take a moment to reflect on a past conflict and write a letter to your spouse. Be specific about what you're apologizing for and how you plan to make things right. This exercise can be cathartic and help clarify your thoughts, making the apology more meaningful. On the flip side, engage in reflective discussions about past conflicts. Talk openly about what happened, what you've learned, and how you can grow from the experience. These conversations foster understanding and pave the way for reconciliation.

In the grand tapestry of relationships, apologies and forgiveness are the threads that weave through every conflict and misunderstanding. They create a pattern of resilience and love that can withstand the test of time. As you navigate the ups and downs of your relationship, remember that it's not about being perfect but about being willing to learn and grow together. With each sincere apology and act of forgiveness, you strengthen your bond, creating a dynamic and enduring union.

As we close this chapter, it's clear that communication—through apologies, forgiveness, listening, and understanding—is the heartbeat of any relationship. It's the foundation upon which everything else is built. As we move forward, remember that each conversation is an opportunity to connect and grow closer, no matter how difficult. And with that, we turn the page to explore how deepening faith can further enrich your relationship, adding another layer of strength and unity.

# CHAPTER 3
# DEEPENING FAITH TOGETHER

Now, let's talk about the importance of this spiritual tag team. You and your spouse are each other's biggest cheerleaders, including cheering each other on your faith journeys. Whether it's a church service, a retreat, or a seminar, these gatherings offer a chance to learn, grow, and connect with others who share your beliefs. And let's not forget the power of sharing personal spiritual insights and reflections. These conversations can be like a warm cup of cocoa for the soul, nurturing your connection and deepening your understanding of each other's spiritual paths.

But let's be honest; no one likes to be pushed into something they're not ready for. Encouraging growth without pressure is key. It's like nudging your spouse to try a new dish without force-feeding it to them. Suggesting books or sermons that resonate with shared values can be a gentle way to inspire spiritual curiosity. Drop hints about a great podcast, leave a book on the coffee table, and let them discover it at their own pace. Celebrating spiritual milestones together is another fantastic way to foster growth. Whether it's a baptism anniversary, a personal breakthrough, or completing a study series, these moments are worth acknowledging. They're like spiritual birthdays that deserve a little fanfare or a cupcake.

Growing together in faith brings a plethora of benefits to your relationship. It builds a deeper emotional and spiritual connection, creating a bond as strong as that weird glue they use in space. When you share your faith, you're not just connecting on a surface level but diving into something profound and meaningful. This shared spiritual journey also creates a supportive environment for individual growth. It's like having a personal cheering squad that's always got your back, encouraging you to explore and expand your faith without judgment.

So, how do you promote mutual spiritual development? Engaging in couple's retreats or spiritual workshops can be an excellent way to start. These experiences offer a chance to step away from the daily grind and focus on your spiritual connection. When we implemented the Couples Ministry at Ebenezer, we would go on a yearly retreat to remind the couples that outside their responsibilities as providers and parents, they were still men and women who needed time for each other. That retreat weekend was designated for the couples to rekindle their husband/wife time, often lost because of schedules and obligations. Picture a spa day where you both emerge refreshed and rejuvenated. Participating in volunteer work is another powerful way to grow together in faith. Serving others reflects your values and strengthens your bond as you work for a common cause. It's an opportunity to live out your faith in action, showing love and compassion to the world around you.

*Spiritual Growth Checklist*

Consider creating a checklist to track your shared spiritual activities and goals. Include items like establishing a membership with a local congregation and participating in weekly bible study or ministry activities. Use this checklist as a guide to keep your spiritual growth on track and celebrate your achievements.

In the tapestry of life, faith is the thread that weaves everything together, creating a beautiful and resilient pattern. As you walk this path together, remember that each step forward is a testament to your commitment to each other and the divine.

## 3.1 DAILY DEVOTIONAL TIME: MAKING SCRIPTURE A SHARED JOURNEY

Imagine starting each day not with the frantic rush of alarms and emails but with a moment of tranquility shared with your spouse. A daily devotional is a consistent time to connect with God. Think of it as a daily check-in, a touchstone that brings your focus back to what truly matters. Regular devotionals strengthen your faith by creating a rhythm that centers you and provides comfort, like a favorite song. Setting a consistent time for these devotionals is key —whether it's morning coffee or winding down in the evening, find what works for both of you. The routine becomes a sacred ritual, a reliable space for reflection and growth.

Start by selecting devotional materials that speak to both of your hearts. I recommend a Daily Bread publication with daily reflections, or perhaps you prefer a podcast that sparks conversation. The important thing is that it feels right for both of you. Next, create a peaceful, distraction-free space to engage with the material and each other fully. Consider it your sanctuary, even if it's a cozy living room corner.

Scripture holds the power to transform and deepen your bond. When you read and discuss it together, you're not just absorbing words on a page; you're sharing insights and interpretations that can illuminate new paths in your relationship. It's like unlocking hidden doors to understanding and empathy. Reflecting on how scriptures apply to your challenges can be enlightening. Maybe a passage about patience speaks to a recent disagreement, or a story of forgiveness helps heal a lingering hurt. These discussions can be profound, offering fresh perspectives and solutions to your issues. It's about seeing scripture as a living, breathing guide that walks with you through every season of life.

Devotional practices are as diverse as the couples who engage in them. One approach is using a journal to document your reflections and prayers. Think of it as a shared diary where your thoughts and hopes intertwine, creating a beautiful tapestry of your spiritual journey. Another option is to incorporate music or art into your devotional experience. Maybe you listen to a worship song that inspires you or creates art that reflects your reflections. These creative elements can enrich the experience, making it more engaging and personal. It's about finding what sparks joy and connection for both of you.

### *Reflection Section: Creating Your Devotional Space*

Take a moment to discuss with your spouse how you envision your devotional time. What materials excite you? How can you make your environment more inviting? Consider jotting down your ideas and setting a date to create your sacred space together.

In the end, daily devotionals are about carving out a time when you can be fully present with each other and God's Word. As you engage in this practice, you'll find that it becomes a cherished part of your day, a moment that nourishes your relationship and your faith. Whether you're reading scripture, listening to music, or simply sitting in silence, these moments are a testament to your commitment to each other and the divine.

## 3.2 PRAYER WARRIORS: STRENGTHENING YOUR RELATIONSHIP THROUGH PRAYER

Ah, prayer—sometimes it feels like the Swiss Army knife of spiritual tools. It's versatile, always there when you need it, and somehow manages to fix things you didn't even know were broken. When you pray together as a couple, you're building trust and intimacy through a shared vulnerability. Envision two people, eyes closed, hearts open, revealing their deepest hopes and fears to God and each other. It's like opening a window to your soul, inviting your spouse to see the view. This shared vulnerability fosters a connection beyond the physical, creating a spiritual bond that strengthens the entire relationship. It's a moment where you both stand on sacred ground, united in purpose and hope.

But how do you make joint prayer a regular part of your life without turning it into another item on your to-do list? The secret lies in establishing a prayer schedule that fits both spouses. Maybe mornings work best, or perhaps evening prayers help you wind down and reflect on the day. Find what suits your rhythm and stick to it. Consistency is key, but flexibility is your friend. Thankfulness is like the seasoning that flavors your prayers, reminding you of your blessings, while requests are your heart's desires laid bare before

God. It's a balance of acknowledging the now and hoping for the future.

Now, let's talk about the elephant in the room—conflict. Yes, even the most harmonious couples have disagreements. Here's where prayer can be a game-changer. Imagine you're in a heated debate about something trivial, like caring for a pet. Instead of letting it spiral into World War III, what if you paused to pray for guidance and wisdom? It shifts the focus from winning an argument to seeking peace and understanding. Prayer helps you navigate disputes gracefully and patiently, reminding you both that you're on the same team. Seeking divine intervention can diffuse tension, opening the door to resolution and reconciliation.

There are various forms of prayer to explore, each offering its unique flavor of connection. Praying aloud together can be an empowering experience. It's about voicing your intentions, hopes, and struggles, letting your spouse hear the melody of your faith. Writing prayer requests and answers in a shared journal can be profoundly meaningful for those who prefer a more introspective approach. This practice creates a tangible record of your spiritual journey together, a testament to the power of prayer in your relationship. It's like leaving a breadcrumb trail of hope and faith that you can reflect on during challenging times.

### *Call to Action: Start a Prayer Journal*

Consider starting a shared prayer journal with your spouse. Dedicate a section for gratitude and another for requests, and leave space for recording answered prayers. Make it a weekly ritual to reflect on these entries together, celebrating the growth and blessings from shared prayer.

In the grand orchestra of life, prayer is the melody that brings harmony to your relationship. The thread weaves through every interaction, lifting you to peace and unity. As you embrace this practice, you'll find that prayer strengthens your bond and infuses your relationship with a sense of divine purpose and love. Whether whispered in the quiet of dawn or spoken aloud under the stars, your prayers are a powerful testament to the passion and commitment you share.

## 3.3 FAITH IN ACTION: LIVING OUT BIBLICAL PRINCIPLES DAILY

Living your faith isn't just about the big gestures; it's about the little actions that reflect love and compassion in everyday interactions. Picture it as sprinkling kindness like confetti wherever you go. Biblical teachings invite us to treat others with the same care and respect we wish for ourselves. This means that how you talk to your spouse, the smile you give to a stranger, or the patience you show in traffic are all opportunities to demonstrate love. It's about letting your faith shine through in the mundane moments, turning the ordinary into extraordinary reflections of divine love.

Incorporating faith into your daily routine can be as simple as starting each day with a scripture reflection. It's like giving your soul a wake-up call before tackling the day's challenges. Find a quiet moment to read a verse or passage that resonates with you, and let its wisdom guide your actions and mindset. Additionally, practicing acts of kindness can be a beautiful expression of your faith. These small gestures can significantly impact you, whether holding the door for someone, paying a compliment, or volunteering your time. They're like little love notes from God, reminding others

—and yourself—that they are valued and loved. Integrating these practices into your day-to-day life creates a rhythm that aligns with your values, making faith a natural part of who you are.

Faith is like a gentle breeze that influences the dynamics of your relationship, encouraging patience and understanding even in disagreements. Faith reminds you to take a step back, breathe, and approach the situation gracefully when tensions rise. It's about choosing empathy over anger and solutions over blame. Supporting each other's goals becomes a natural extension of this mindset as you cheer each other on with faith-based encouragement. Imagine being each other's biggest fans, rooted in the belief that together, you can achieve great things. This support isn't just about words; it's about actions that reflect your commitment to each other's growth and happiness.

Consider setting weekly intentions based on biblical teachings to put faith into action. This isn't about lofty goals but small, achievable steps that align with your values. Perhaps it's focusing on gratitude, practicing patience, or finding joy in the journey. These intentions serve as gentle reminders to live purposefully, guided by your faith. Another powerful way to live out your faith is through volunteering together. Find a cause that resonates with both of you and dedicate time to serving others. Whether it's helping at a local food bank, participating in community clean-ups, or mentoring youth, these acts of service strengthen your bond and reflect the love and compassion central to your faith. Remember, "faith without works is dead."

Faith in action is about embracing your beliefs in your daily life, transforming each moment into an opportunity to let your little light shine. It's about letting your actions speak louder than words, creating opportunities to share love and kindness with everyone around you. As you embrace these practices, you'll find that your faith shapes who you are and enriches the relationships that matter most. Whether through small acts of kindness or more significant gestures of service, living your faith is a testimony of your belief.

## 3.4 SPIRITUAL ARMOR: PROTECTING YOUR RELATIONSHIP WITH FAITH

Have you ever thought about faith as a form of armor? Not the clunky medieval kind that makes you clatter down the hallway, but a protective force that shields your relationship from the inevitable storms of life. This spiritual armor isn't something you put on and forget about. It's a living, breathing part of your relationship that builds resilience against external challenges. Think of it as a warm, invisible cloak that wraps around you and your spouse, offering protection and strength. Life can throw curveballs, be it stress from work, family pressures, or personal struggles. But with faith as your armor, you're fortified against these challenges, able to stand firm and united.

Strengthening this spiritual armor requires intentionality. One powerful way to enhance your spiritual defenses is by regularly studying and memorizing scripture. Consider it sharpening your spiritual sword, equipping you with wisdom and guidance for whatever comes your way. Dive into the Word together, and let it speak to your hearts. Memorization may feel like a throwback to school days, but it's more about allowing the scriptures to become a part of you, ready to be drawn upon in times of need. Another strategy is engaging in communal worship. There's something profoundly uplifting about joining others in prayer and feeling a community's collective faith and support. It's like a spiritual recharge, filling your well so you can pour into each other. Surrounding yourselves with fellow believers creates a network of support, a safety net that catches you when you stumble.

When adversity strikes, faith becomes the beacon that guides you through the storm. Challenges are inevitable, but they don't have to be insurmountable. Scripture strengthens during difficult times, reminding you of promises and truths that anchor you. In these moments, the words you've studied and memorized become life-lines, whispering hope and courage into your heart. Relying on prayer as a comfort and guidance can transform even the darkest nights. It's about turning to God in uncertain moments, trusting His light will lead you through. Prayer becomes the dialogue that sustains you, offering reassurance and clarity when the path seems unclear.

Let's talk about practical ways to apply this spiritual protection. Consider creating a prayer shield for your relationship. This could be a dedicated time each day or week where you pray specifically for your marriage, asking for strength, wisdom, and protection. It's like a protective bubble surrounding your relationship, reinforcing your bond. Another idea is establishing a support network within your faith community. Having a support network is invaluable, whether it's a small group, a prayer circle, or simply a few trusted friends. Prayer warriors stand with you, pray for you, and offer encouragement when needed. They become the armor bearers who help carry your burdens, offering strength and solidarity.

As we wrap up this chapter, remember that spiritual armor is not just a shield; it's a source of strength that empowers you to face life's challenges with courage and conviction. It's about being proactive and equipping yourself with steadfast and unshakeable faith. With this armor, you're not just protecting your relationship but nurturing it, allowing it to flourish even in adversity. As we move forward, consider how this armor can continue to shape and strengthen your relationship, preparing you for whatever lies ahead.

# CHAPTER 4
# CONFLICT RESOLUTION TOOLS

In marriage, conflicts are no laughing matter—they're inevitable. They can spring from the most mundane issues; if you're not careful, they can snowball into something more. Understanding the root causes of conflict is crucial for navigating these choppy waters without sinking the ship.

One common source of friction is differing communication styles and expectations. You might think you're being transparent, but it's like trying to watch a foreign film without subtitles if your spouse is on a different wavelength. One person might enjoy long, detailed discussions, while the other prefers quick, to-the-point exchanges. Without recognizing this difference, conversations can become frustrating, leading to misunderstandings. Then there's financial stress, a classic culprit. Budgeting disagreements can turn even the calmest household into a financial battleground. Whether deciding on a big purchase or simply arguing over a coffee habit, money matters can strain even the most substantial relationships. And let's not forget family and in-law dynamics, those delightful minefields of opinions and traditions. Navigating these relationships can feel like walking a tightrope, balancing respect for each other's families while maintaining your boundaries.

Beneath these surface issues often lie deeper emotional triggers. Past traumas can color our reactions, turning a simple disagreement into a replay of old wounds. Maybe it's a childhood experience or a previous relationship that casts a long shadow. Fear of vulnerability or rejection can also rear its head, making it hard to open up or accept criticism fully. When we feel exposed, our defenses go up, and a simple comment can feel like a personal attack. Recognizing these emotional undercurrents is key to addressing conflict effectively.

Patterns in arguments can be as predictable as your favorite sitcom's plot twists. Perhaps every disagreement starts with a similar complaint or ends in the same unresolved silence. Recognizing these patterns is like spotting a plot twist before it happens. Stress and fatigue often play a role, too. When running on empty, patience wears thin, and even minor irritations can ignite a spark. Identifying these recurring issues is the first step toward breaking the cycle and finding more constructive communication methods.

### *Reflection Exercise: Mapping Conflict Patterns*

Take some time to reflect on your most common arguments. What themes or triggers keep popping up? Consider journaling about these patterns, noting how stress or fatigue might influence them. This exercise can help you pinpoint the underlying causes and shift your approach.

Self-awareness is a powerful tool in conflict resolution. By journaling about emotions and triggers, you can clarify what sets you off and why. Writing down your feelings can be cathartic, helping you process emotions before they boil over. Mindfulness practices can also enhance your self-awareness, allowing you to stay present and recognize your emotional state. It's like having an internal thermostat that alerts you when the temperature rises, allowing you to cool down before things get heated. By embracing these tools, you can navigate conflicts with greater understanding and empathy, building a stronger, more resilient relationship.

## 4.1 CONSTRUCTIVE CONFLICT: TURNING DISAGREEMENTS INTO GROWTH OPPORTUNITIES

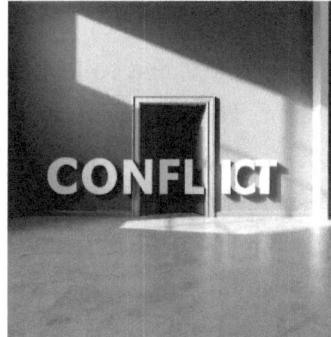

You know that feeling when a disagreement seems to hover in the air like a storm cloud, ready to unleash its fury? It's easy to see conflict as an opposing force, but what if I told you it could catalyze positive change? Imagine, for a moment, that each disagreement holds the potential to deepen under- standing and empathy between you and your spouse. It's like finding a hidden gem amid the rubble. When we approach conflict with curiosity rather than defensiveness, we open the door to learning more about each other's perspectives. This deeper under- standing can strengthen your bond, making it more resilient and adaptable. Additionally, navigating these conflicts can hone your problem-solving skills. Each argument becomes an opportunity to practice finding creative solutions, turning what could be a stumbling block into a stepping stone.

Establishing ground rules for respectful communication is helpful to keep discussions productive. Picture it as setting the rules for a game, ensuring everyone plays fair. These might include agreeing to let each person speak without interruption or committing to a time-out if emotions run high. These rules create a safe environment where both spouses feel heard and respected. Another technique is to focus on solutions rather than assigning blame. Instead of getting stuck in a cycle of "It's your fault," shift the conversation to "How can we fix this together?" This change in focus encourages collaboration, turning a potential battleground into a brainstorming session. It's about working as a team, not as opponents. When both spouses are committed to finding a resolution, the outcome is often more satisfying and constructive.

Compromise and collaboration are the cornerstones of conflict resolution. Think of them as the secret ingredients in your relationship recipe, adding flavor and depth. Finding common ground in disagreements involves looking beyond the immediate issue to see the bigger picture. It's about recognizing shared goals and values that unite you, even when opinions differ. Focusing on these commonalities can transform a divisive issue into a unifying experience. Exploring win-win solutions that satisfy both spouses is another essential strategy. It's like crafting a dish that satisfies your sweet tooth and your spouse's savory cravings. These solutions require creativity and flexibility, creating a more harmonious and balanced relationship.

Consider the story of a couple who faced differences in parenting styles. She was all about structure and rules, while he favored a more laid-back approach. Initially, their conversations were tense, each trying to convince the other of their perspective. However, by focusing on their shared goal of raising happy, healthy children, they were able to find common ground. They blended their styles, incorporating structure and flexibility into their parenting. This compromise resolved their conflict and strengthened their marriage as parents. In another case, a couple disagreed over financial planning. One preferred saving for the future, while the other wanted to enjoy the present. Instead of letting this become a point of contention, they sat down to explore options that could satisfy both needs. They decided to allocate a portion of their budget for savings while setting aside some for spontaneous adventures. This approach addressed their financial concerns and enriched their relationship by fostering collaboration and understanding.

## 4.2 GRACE AND PATIENCE: APPROACHING CONFLICT WITH A CHRIST-LIKE ATTITUDE

Engaging in godly communications, "slow to wrath and swift to listen," is a Christ-like approach to conflict that will improve a relationship. At the heart of this approach lie spiritual virtues like forgiveness and understanding, which are as essential as air and water in resolving conflicts. Forgiveness is the gentle reminder that we all stumble and need grace. It's not about ignoring the wrong but choosing to love and heal despite it. On the other hand, understanding is akin to looking through a window into your spouse's world, seeking to comprehend their perspective rather than just your own. The Bible teaches us to clothe ourselves with compassion and kindness; these virtues are the threads that weave through every successful conflict resolution. Humility and empathy also play crucial roles. Humility allows us to admit we're wrong, and empathy helps us feel what our spouse feels, fostering a deeper connection.

Patience is another key component, and boy, is it meaningful! Patience is like the soothing balm over a heated argument, giving time and space for emotions to settle. Have you ever tried untangling a knot in a rush? It usually just tightens. The same goes for resolving disputes. Allowing emotions to cool before addressing issues can prevent words from being spoken in haste and actions from being taken too quickly. It's like letting a stew simmer until just right, ensuring that you're both ready to engage thoughtfully when you finally sit down to discuss. Patience allows us to wait, listen, and understand without rushing to conclusions. This measured approach often leads to more meaningful and less heated conversations where both spouses feel heard and respected.

Cultivating grace in our interactions isn't just a lofty ideal; it's a practice we can develop. Reflecting on biblical teachings about love and grace can be a powerful reminder of how we're called to act. This might mean spending a few moments each day reading passages that speak to the heart of love, kindness, and patience. These reflections can guide your actions and attitudes, grounding them in a more profound spiritual truth. Practicing active gratitude during challenging times is another way to embody grace. When tension arises, it's easy to focus on the negatives, but consciously recognizing and appreciating the positives can shift the energy in a relationship. It's like shining a light into the dark corners, revealing the good that might go unnoticed.

To develop patience and grace further, consider some practical exercises. Breathing exercises are a simple yet effective way to maintain calmness during heated moments. Just a few deep breaths can help center your thoughts and emotions, providing clarity and calm. Prayer and meditation focused on patience can also be transformative. Set aside time to pray for patience, asking for guidance in navigating conflicts with love and empathy. Meditation, even for a few minutes each day, can quiet the mind and nurture a sense of peace that you can draw upon when needed. These practices are more than just techniques; they're acts of love and commitment to nurturing a relationship that reflects the beauty and grace of a Christ-centered marriage.

## 4.3 FINDING PEACE: FAITH-BASED STRATEGIES FOR RESOLUTION

Have you ever noticed how a simple prayer can change the whole vibe of a conversation? It's like adding sugar to bitter coffee. Prayer is one of those faith-based conflict resolution techniques that can bring clarity when everything feels like a tangled mess. It's not just about asking for help; it's about creating a space where you can listen for guidance and wisdom. Imagine sitting together, holding hands, and inviting God into the conversation. It's as if you're adding a third, all-knowing party to your discussion, someone who sees the bigger picture and helps you navigate through the noise. Inviting God in can turn a heated argument into a moment of reflection and understanding, allowing both spouses to feel heard and validated.

Scripture is another powerful tool for finding peace. The Bible is filled with passages that offer guidance on peacemaking and reconciliation. Take Romans 12:18, for example, where it says, "If it is possible, as far as it depends on you, live at peace with everyone." This reminds us that while we can't control everything, we can strive for peace. The Apostle Paul in his letter to Philippians (Philippians 4:7) wrote about peace saying, *"And the peace of God, which passeth all understanding, shall keep your hearts and minds through Christ Jesus."* We got to have Jesus. Reflecting on stories of forgiveness and redemption can also be enlightening. Consider the Prodigal Son, who was welcomed back with open arms despite his mistakes. Such stories teach us that forgiveness isn't just a gift we give others; it's a path to healing our own hearts. By studying these passages, you gain insight into how to handle conflicts with grace and compassion, transforming them into opportunities for growth.

Implementing faith-based strategies can be incredibly rewarding. Start by setting aside time for joint prayer and reflection. It doesn't have to be a grand gesture—a few quiet moments each day can make a world of difference. This time allows you to reconnect with each other and with your faith, creating a foundation of understanding before addressing any issues. Creating a peace plan that includes spiritual practices is another effective approach. Think of it like a roadmap, guiding you through the rough patches with faith as your compass. This plan might include regular scripture study, prayer, and even meditative practices that ground you in your relationship. By incorporating these elements, you create a structured yet flexible approach to resolving conflicts, one that respects both your spiritual and relational needs.

I remember hearing about a couple who faced constant tension over financial disagreements. Instead of letting it fester, they decided to approach the issue with prayer. Every week, they would sit together and pray for guidance, asking God to help them see each other's perspectives. Over time, they found that their conversations became less about winning and more about understanding. Prayer allowed them to see their finances not as a battleground but as a shared responsibility. Another couple I knew struggled with resentment after a particularly hurtful argument. They turned to scripture, reading passages on forgiveness and redemption. As they reflected on these teachings, they found the strength to let go of their anger, opening the door to healing and reconciliation. By leaning on their faith, these couples transformed conflict into connection, showing that peace is not just a possibility but a promise when God is at the center.

## 4.4 HEALING WOUNDS: RESTORING TRUST AFTER CONFLICT

Have you ever tried to glue back together a shattered vase? It can feel like an impossible task, with all the tiny pieces scattered everywhere. Healing after a conflict in a relationship can feel much the same. The key to putting things back together is acknowledging the hurt feelings and offering a sincere apology. This isn't just a matter of saying "I'm sorry" out of obligation. It's about genuinely recognizing the pain caused and conveying a heartfelt apology that reflects understanding and remorse. Once the apology is made, the work of rebuilding trust begins. This requires continuous effort, akin to watering a delicate plant. Trust doesn't magically reappear overnight. It's cultivated through consistent actions that demonstrate reliability and support. Your spouse needs to see that you're committed to change, that you value the relationship enough to put in the necessary work. This ongoing commitment is what ultimately restores intimacy and connection.

Forgiveness plays a crucial role in this healing process. It's the bridge that connects the past with the future, allowing couples to move forward without the heavy baggage of resentment. However, it's important to differentiate between forgiveness and forgetting. Forgiving doesn't mean erasing the memory of what happened. It's about choosing not to let that memory dictate the future of the relationship. It's a conscious decision to release the grip of anger and hurt, making space for healing and growth. Mutual understanding and acceptance are essential here. Both spouses must acknowledge their roles in the conflict and be willing to accept each other's apologies. This mutual recognition fosters an environment where emotional recovery can take root. It's about creating a shared narrative that acknowledges past mistakes while focusing on future possibilities.

To restore confidence in the relationship, setting clear boundaries and expectations is essential. Picture it as establishing a roadmap that guides your interactions. These boundaries help prevent future misunderstandings, providing a framework for how you both wish to be treated. Consistently demonstrating reliability is another powerful step. Follow through on promises, be there when you say you will, and show your spouse that they can count on you. Support isn't just about grand gestures; it's found in the everyday actions that say, "I'm here, and I've got your back." These steps gradually rebuild the foundation of trust, paving the way for a stronger, more connected relationship.

Post-conflict, engaging in shared activities can be a balm for wounded hearts. Whether it's cooking a meal together, taking a walk in nature, or pursuing a shared hobby, these activities offer opportunities to reconnect and rediscover the joy in each other's company. They serve as reminders of what initially drew you together, reigniting the spark that may have dimmed during the conflict. Creating a future vision together is another powerful exercise. Sit down and discuss your hopes and dreams, both individually and as a couple. This shared vision reinforces your commitment to one another, providing a roadmap for the future. It's about dreaming together and building a life that reflects your shared values and aspirations.

As we wrap up Chapter 4, remember that conflict, while challenging, is an opportunity for growth and connection. By embracing forgiveness, rebuilding trust, and fostering intimacy, couples can emerge from conflict stronger and more united. With clear boundaries and shared goals, you lay the groundwork for a fulfilling and lasting relationship. Turning the page, we'll explore how to deepen intimacy and connection, adding another layer to the foundation we've built.

# CHAPTER 5
# FOSTERING INTIMACY AND CONNECTION

I magine your relationship as a cozy old sweater—it's warm, familiar, and something you turn to for comfort. But even the most cherished sweater needs a little care to stay cozy and snug. That's where intimacy comes in, the threads that hold your relationship together, making it more than just a marriage but a shared journey through life. Intimacy isn't just about the grand gestures, like romantic weekends or candlelit dinners, though those are delightful. Adult time between the man and his woman is important and necessary. Only the man can make the wife feel like a woman and only the woman can make the man feel like a man. Intimacy is necessary in marriage. Remember: Adam and Eve's responsibilities were too multiply and be fruitful. So, let's dive into the wonderful world of emotional intimacy, where vulnerability and trust are the stitches that keep your relationship sweater from unraveling.

## 5.1 EMOTIONAL INTIMACY: SHARING VULNERABILITIES AND BUILDING TRUST

Emotional intimacy is like the secret ingredient in your grandma's famous pie—without it, everything else just falls flat. At its core, emotional intimacy is about sharing vulnerabilities, those tender parts of your soul that you usually keep tucked away. By opening up about fears, insecurities, and dreams, you create a deep bond with your spouse. This sharing fosters a connection that goes beyond words, allowing you to truly understand and support each other. It's a bit like peeling an onion, layer by layer, revealing more of yourself to someone you trust. And yes, there might be tears involved, but they're the kind that brings you closer.

Now, encouraging open dialogues about your fears and insecurities can be daunting, like standing on stage with your heart on your sleeve. But creating a safe and supportive environment for sharing makes all the difference. Think of it as building a cozy nest where both of you can feel secure enough to express your thoughts without fear of judgment. Start small, sharing little snippets of your day or discussing minor worries, and gradually work up to more significant topics. It's like dipping your toes into a chilly pool before taking the plunge. Over time, this openness becomes second nature, strengthening the trust and intimacy between you.

Enhancing emotional connection requires more than just talking; it's about truly listening and being present. Practicing empathy and active listening in conversations is like tuning into your favorite song, fully absorbing every note and lyric. When your spouse shares something, listen with your heart as well as your ears. Let them know that what they're saying matters and that you're there for them. Using affirmations is another powerful tool. Express appreciation and love regularly, not just on special occasions. It's like watering a plant; consistent care helps it flourish. Tell your spouse what you love about them and why they're special to you. These affirmations are like little love notes that keep the romance alive.

Of course, building emotional intimacy isn't without its challenges. Fear of judgment or rejection can be a formidable barrier, keeping you locked in a cycle of superficial interactions. But overcoming this fear is like breaking out of a cocoon, emerging stronger and more connected. Encourage gradual sharing of personal stories and experiences. It's not about baring your soul all at once but taking small steps towards deeper sharing. Each story shared is a brick in the foundation of trust, creating a solid base for your relationship.

### *Exercise: Trust-Building Activities*

Try engaging in activities designed to foster trust and openness. One fun exercise is the blindfold walk. Take turns guiding each other around your home or backyard while one spouse wears a blindfold. This activity requires trust and communication, reinforcing your connection. Another idea is to share personal goals and dreams, discussing how you can support each other in achieving them. These exercises are like the threads that weave through your relationship, creating a beautiful tapestry of trust and understanding.

## 5.2 SPIRITUAL INTIMACY: GROWING CLOSER TO GOD AND EACH OTHER

Imagine spiritual intimacy as the invisible thread that ties you and your spouse not only to each other but also to something greater. It's like a secret handshake you share with the universe, binding your relationship with shared beliefs and values. This kind of closeness transcends the everyday, bringing a sense of unity that makes your bond feel unbreakable. It's not just about sitting together in church on Sundays, though that's a lovely part of it. It's about experiencing faith-based activities that resonate with both your hearts, turning ordinary moments into sacred ones. Sharing these experiences fosters a type of intimacy that gives your relationship depth and strength, grounding you in a shared purpose that goes beyond the mundane.

Building this spiritual connection requires intentional effort and a willingness to explore faith together. Regular prayer as a couple is like planting seeds in a garden. With each prayer, you nurture your relationship's spiritual foundation, encouraging mutual growth and understanding. These moments of shared reflection can be as simple as a quiet prayer before meals or as structured as setting aside time each week to pray for each other's needs and dreams. Discussing theological questions and insights is another way to deepen this connection. Imagine it as a spiritual book club, where each discussion brings new insights and perspectives. Whether it's pondering the mysteries of life or exploring how faith shapes your values, these conversations are a treasure trove of discovery and connection, enriching your relationship with every word.

The benefits of spiritual intimacy are profound. Couples who cultivate this type of closeness often find a strengthened sense of purpose and unity. Your shared faith acts like a compass, guiding you through life's challenges with a clear sense of direction. When storms arise, this unity becomes your anchor, providing a safe harbor of support and love. It's about having each other's backs, knowing that no matter what, you're in it together. Spiritual intimacy also enhances support during spiritual challenges. When one of you struggles with doubt or uncertainty, the other becomes a source of reassurance and strength. This mutual support fosters resilience, allowing you to face adversity with confidence and grace.

To develop spiritual intimacy further, consider engaging in activities that bring you closer to God and each other. A couple's Bible study or faith group is a fantastic way to start. These gatherings offer a space to explore scripture together, sparking discussions that deepen your understanding and connection. Being part of a faith community also provides valuable support, surrounding you with others who share your values and can offer encouragement. Another enriching exercise is creating a shared spiritual vision or mission statement. This isn't about drafting a manifesto but capturing what matters most to you both spiritually. Discuss your shared goals and values, and put them into words that inspire and guide your relationship. This vision serves as a beacon, reminding you of your shared path and the love that binds you.

## 5.3 PHYSICAL INTIMACY: CELEBRATING THE GIFT OF TOGETHERNESS

Physical intimacy is like the glue that holds the pages of your love story together. It's the warm embrace after a long day, the gentle touch that reassures, and the closeness that speaks volumes without saying a word. In a healthy relationship, physical intimacy plays a pivotal role in enhancing the emotional bond. It's not just about the physical act itself but about expressing love and affection in a tangible way. Holding hands, hugging, or even a simple touch on the shoulder can strengthen your connection, making you feel seen, valued, and cherished. These small acts of affection are the heartbeat of a relationship, keeping it alive and vibrant. They serve as reminders of the love you share, deepening your bond and fostering a sense of security and warmth.

To nurture physical intimacy, go to Victoria Secrets and purchase the appropriate outfits to enhance closeness. Scheduling regular intimate time without distractions is crucial. Think of it as setting a date with your favorite person, where the world fades away, and it's just the two of you. Whether it's a quiet evening or a lazy Saturday morning, make it a priority. During this time, explore new ways to express physical affection. Maybe it's trying out a new dance class together, where you can twirl and dip to your heart's content, or perhaps it's finding quiet moments for a spontaneous hug or kiss. These gestures, however small, build a tapestry of love and connection, one that grows richer with each shared moment.

Of course, physical intimacy isn't without its challenges. Stress and fatigue can often impact desire, turning what should be a joyful experience into another item on the to-do list. To combat this, focus on managing stress effectively. Perhaps it's unwinding with a warm bath together or taking a leisurely walk hand in hand. Open communication about needs and preferences is also vital. Discuss what you both enjoy and what you'd like more or less of in your intimate life. This openness creates an environment where both spouses feel comfortable and respected, paving the way for a fulfilling physical connection. Spontaneous intimacy will give the relationship the energy needed in challenging times.

To celebrate physical togetherness, consider engaging in activities that bring you closer. Planning surprise romantic evenings or getaways can reignite the spark. Picture a cozy cabin in the woods, a picnic under the stars, or simply a candlelit dinner at home. These moments offer a break from routine, allowing you to focus solely on each other. Regular physical activities together, like dancing or yoga, also enhance intimacy. These activities encourage teamwork, trust, and a shared sense of accomplishment. Plus, they're a lot of fun! Whether you're learning a new dance step or perfecting a yoga pose, these experiences foster a deeper connection, blending physical closeness with shared joy.

## 5.4 DATE NIGHT: NURTURING YOUR RELATIONSHIP WITH INTENTIONAL TIME

Imagine date night as the secret ingredient in the recipe of a thriving relationship. It's that special time when you hit pause on the hustle and bustle of life and focus solely on each other. Regular date nights are crucial because they reinforce your commitment and prioritize your relationship. They provide the perfect opportunity to reconnect and relax, like slipping into a warm bath after a long day. In a world where schedules are packed and distractions are endless, date nights are the oasis in the desert, reminding you why you chose each other in the first place. These evenings are about more than just dining out; they're a celebration of your togetherness, a time to laugh, talk, and simply be.

Now, let's talk about spicing things up with creative date ideas that keep the spark alive. Cooking a meal together from a new cuisine is a delightful way to bond. Picture both of you in the kitchen, clumsily chopping ingredients and sneaking tastes as you go along. Whether it's a spicy Thai curry or a delicate French soufflé, the joy is in the shared experience—mistakes and all. Exploring local attractions or attending cultural events offers a change of scenery and new experiences. Whether it's a visit to a quirky museum, a stroll through a botanical garden, or attending a community theater production, these outings provide a refreshing break from routine. They're the perfect backdrop for making memories and sparking conversations that go beyond the usual "How was your day?"

Of course, getting these date nights on the calendar can feel like trying to fit a square peg in a round hole. Busy schedules and family responsibilities often hijack your plans, leaving little room for romance. This is where setting boundaries becomes your best ally. Protecting date night time means saying no to other commitments occasionally, even if it feels uncomfortable. Think of it as guarding a treasure, because that's exactly what it is—precious time for just the two of you. Consider creating a shared calendar to keep track of your plans. It's like having a relationship planner that ensures you're both on the same page. By marking out your date nights in advance, you make them a priority, just like any other important meeting or event.

Maintaining consistency with date nights requires a bit of creativity and teamwork. Alternating planning responsibilities between spouses keeps things fresh and exciting. One week it's your turn to surprise your spouse, and the next, it's theirs. This way, you both get to inject your unique personalities and interests into your dates, keeping the anticipation alive. Maybe you plan a cozy movie night at home, complete with popcorn and a blanket fort, while your spouse takes you out for a night of stargazing. The key is to keep the excitement bubbling, ensuring that date nights remain a cherished highlight in your relationship.

So, as you embark on this delightful adventure of regular date nights, remember that it's not about perfection. It's about connection. It's about taking those precious moments to look into each other's eyes and remember why you fell in love. So go ahead, plan that quirky outing or cook up a storm in the kitchen. Whatever you do, do it together.

## 5.5 CULTIVATING GRATITUDE: APPRECIATING YOUR SPOUSE'S UNIQUE GIFTS

Imagine your relationship as a garden, where gratitude acts as the nourishing sunlight and rain that helps everything grow. Expressing appreciation isn't just a polite gesture; it's the foundation of a positive and supportive atmosphere. When you regularly express gratitude, you're telling your spouse, "I see you, and I value you," which fosters mutual respect and admiration. This creates a space where both spouses feel cherished and motivated to continue nurturing the relationship. It's like adding layers to a cake, each one sweeter than the last, and over time, these expressions of gratitude build a solid, satisfying bond. Brethren, you have to actively choose to love your wives. Remember: *"your responsibility is to love your wife as Christ loved the church."*

Expressing gratitude doesn't have to be a grand affair. Sometimes, the simplest gestures are the most profound. Writing gratitude notes or letters is a timeless way to show appreciation. Imagine leaving a note in your spouse's lunchbox or on their bedside table, expressing how much you admire their kindness or how grateful you are for their support. These notes serve as little reminders of love that your spouse can carry with them throughout the day. Verbalizing specific qualities or actions you admire can be just as impactful. A heartfelt "Thank you for being so patient with me today," or "I love how you always make me laugh," can turn an ordinary moment into a cherished memory. These verbal affirmations are like verbal hugs, wrapping your spouse in warmth and appreciation.

The impact of gratitude on relationship dynamics is profound. Regular appreciation increases overall happiness and satisfaction, like a shot of espresso for the soul. It shifts the focus from what might be lacking to what is already abundant, reducing resentment and negative feelings. Gratitude acts as a buffer against the everyday stresses and strains, reminding you both of the good that exists even during challenging times. It's like having a secret weapon against negativity, one that reinforces the positive aspects of your relationship. Studies have shown that couples who regularly express gratitude spend more time together and report improved satisfaction in their relationships, including their sex lives. Gratitude has a ripple effect, enhancing emotional and social well-being while strengthening the very fabric of your connection.

To cultivate gratitude further, consider engaging in exercises that reinforce appreciation. Keeping a shared gratitude journal is a delightful way to document the things you're thankful for. Take turns writing entries, noting both big and small moments. It could be as simple as enjoying a sunset together or as significant as overcoming a challenge. This journal becomes a testament to the love and gratitude that permeate your relationship, a tangible reminder of the blessings you share. Starting or ending the day with expressions of gratitude is another powerful practice. Whether it's over morning coffee or before drifting off to sleep, take a moment to express what you appreciate about each other. This habit sets a positive tone for the day or wraps it up with warmth, reinforcing the bond between you.

As we wrap up our exploration of intimacy and connection, remember that gratitude is the thread that weaves through every aspect of your relationship. By appreciating each other's unique gifts, you create a marriage that thrives on mutual respect, admiration, and love. Each expression of gratitude is a step towards a deeper, more fulfilling connection, one that stands strong through life's ups and downs. With these foundations in place, turn the page to discover new ways to navigate the challenges that life presents, armed with the love and gratitude that bind you together.

## United By Faith

*"Your marriage is a gift—not just to the two of you, but to this world."*

AARON AND JENNIFER SMITH,
*MARRIAGE AFTER GOD*

I've had many conversations with many couples in my office, but still the one that resonates with me the most is the one I told you about in the introduction. It was the flicker of relief on their faces that they weren't alone that struck me.

Many couples go through the occasional rough patch, but when you're in the middle of it, you feel like you're the only one. Your head starts jumping to conclusions; you panic that you're not going to be able to make it work; you notice feelings of inadequacy creeping in. You forget that countless other couples are going through the same thing, and you feel helpless.

But when you remember that so many other couples have been here before you and turned to their faith to guide them through and find each other again, a glimmer of hope ignites inside you. You realize that between yourselves and your faith, you have everything you need to get you through—and all you need then is a little guidance.

This devotional is here to give you that guidance, but never forget that it's you, your partner, and your faith in God that are doing all the work. Nonetheless, I'd like to make sure it reaches as many of the other couples who need it as possible, and for that, I'd like to ask for your help.

You can help other couples to realize that there are many others like them working on their relationship and strengthening their faith in God by leaving a short note online. You can do that in the form of a review, simultaneously pointing them in the direction of this devotional so that they can easily find the guidance they need.

**By leaving a review of this book on Amazon, you'll show other couples that they're not alone and point them in the direction of the support they're looking for.**

Reviews are powerful tools for starting a conversation around a topic that many people are looking for help with, and a few words from you could make a huge difference to another couple.

Thank you so much for your support. God enables us to do many things, but we're at our most effective when we work together.

# CHAPTER 6
# OVERCOMING SPIRITUAL IMBALANCES

Have you ever tried assembling a piece of IKEA furniture without all the parts? It's frustrating to have mismatched pieces, and it feels like something's missing. Similarly, spiritual imbalances in a relationship can leave you feeling like you're trying to put together a puzzle with missing pieces. You might find that you and your spouse are at different stages in your spiritual journey, and that's okay. It's normal to experience these gaps, but it's important to recognize them and find ways to bridge them.

## 6.1 BRIDGING SPIRITUAL GAPS: UNDERSTANDING DIFFERENT LEVELS OF FAITH

Let's face it: not everyone gets the same thrill from Sunday sermons or feels equally moved by a sunrise meditation. Recognizing the presence of spiritual gaps is the first step in addressing them. You might notice that your spouse exhibits less enthusiasm for faith-based activities, like they're attending out of obligation rather than excitement. Or perhaps they're not as comfortable discussing spiritual topics, preferring to keep their thoughts private. These differences might seem small, but they can create a rift if left unaddressed. It's crucial to observe these signs without judgment, understanding that everyone's faith journey is unique and personal.

Spiritual gaps can affect relationships in various ways. For some, these differences can lead to feelings of frustration or inadequacy, making one spouse feel like they're carrying the spiritual load alone. You might wonder why your spouse doesn't share your passion for certain practices, leading to potential misunderstandings or miscommunication. Imagine trying to have a conversation where one person speaks in metaphors while the other is strictly literal. Without addressing these gaps, you risk drifting apart, each of you on your own spiritual island. However, recognizing these gaps can also open the door to deeper understanding and connection.

Bridging these gaps requires intentional effort and communication. Start by encouraging open conversations about your spiritual needs and expectations. This isn't about converting your spouse to your way of thinking but about understanding where they stand and how you can support each other. Ask questions and listen without judgment, creating a safe space for honest dialogue. Finding shared spiritual activities that both spouses enjoy is another effective strategy. Maybe it's attending a yoga class or exploring a nature trail that feels sacred. The goal is to find common ground that nurtures both of your spirits, allowing you to grow together rather than apart.

### *Reflection Section: Shared Spiritual Exploration*

Consider setting aside time each week for a listening session where each spouse shares their spiritual experiences and insights. Use this time to explore spiritual literature or media that appeals to both of you. This could be a podcast, a book, or even a film that sparks conversation and reflection. These shared explorations can foster empathy and mutual respect, strengthening your connection.

Fostering understanding involves more than just surface-level conversations. It requires diving deeper into each other's spiritual worlds and embracing the differences you find there. Listening sessions are a great starting point. Set aside time regularly to share your spiritual experiences and insights. This isn't about debating whose path is better but about learning from each other's journeys. It's like being a tourist in your spouse's spiritual world, discovering new landscapes and perspectives. Joint exploration of spiritual literature or media can also promote mutual respect and understanding. Choose books, podcasts, or films that intrigue you both, and discuss your thoughts and feelings. These activities can bring you closer, creating a shared spiritual tapestry woven from your individual threads.

In the end, overcoming spiritual imbalances is about embracing the journey together, even when your paths diverge. It's about finding harmony in the differences, using them as opportunities for growth rather than division. With patience, empathy, and open communication, you can bridge the gaps and build a relationship that thrives on both unity and diversity. Remember, the goal isn't to erase the differences but to celebrate and learn from them, creating a marriage that is richer and more fulfilling because of them.

## 6.2 ENCOURAGING SPIRITUAL CURIOSITY: EXPLORING FAITH TOGETHER

Picture this: you're both sitting at the breakfast table, sipping your coffee, and suddenly the topic of spirituality comes up. Perhaps you glance outside and see the birds chirping, the sun rising, and you wonder about the bigger picture. This curiosity, this innate desire to explore beyond your usual boundaries, can be a powerful force in your relationship. Encouraging spiritual curiosity is like opening a treasure chest filled with potential. It invites growth and new perspectives, strengthening your bond through shared discovery. When both spouses are curious and open to learning, it creates a dynamic energy that infuses your relationship with excitement and wonder. Exploring faith together isn't about finding definitive answers. Instead, it's about asking questions, seeking understanding, and allowing your relationship to evolve in unexpected and profound ways.

To spark this curiosity, you might consider introducing diverse spiritual practices or traditions. Imagine trying on different hats to see which one fits best—experimenting with meditation, journaling, or even tai chi. These practices can offer fresh insights and deepen your spiritual connection. Attending interfaith seminars or discussions can also be enlightening. These events provide a platform for exploring varied beliefs and perspectives, allowing you to see the world through a new lens. It's like attending a potluck where everyone brings a different dish. You get to sample a bit of everything, broadening your palate and enriching your understanding. These experiences can break down barriers and open up conversations that you might never have thought to have.

Shared learning opportunities can further enhance your spiritual exploration. Consider enrolling in a theology or spirituality course together. Whether it's online or in-person, these courses offer structured learning and fascinating discussions that can deepen your understanding of each other's beliefs. It's like taking a road trip through the landscape of faith, with each lesson offering a new vista. Alternatively, participating in faith-based book clubs or discussion groups can provide a supportive community for exploring spiritual topics. These groups create a space for dialogue and reflection, allowing you to connect with others who share your interests. Imagine gathering with a group of friends over tea, each of you bringing your own insights and questions to the table. These shared learning experiences can strengthen your bond, providing a foundation for continued growth.

For those who prefer more hands-on exploration, visiting various places of worship can be a profound experience. Each place offers a unique glimpse into different faith traditions and practices. You might find yourself in a serene temple one week and a lively mosque the next, each visit offering new insights and perspectives. It's like being a tourist in the world of spirituality, with each stop on the journey unveiling a new facet of faith. Engaging in spiritual retreats focused on learning and exploration is another option. These retreats provide an immersive experience, allowing you to step away from daily routines and focus on your spiritual growth. Whether it's a silent retreat in the mountains or a weekend workshop in the city, these experiences can be transformative, offering both renewal and inspiration.

### *Call to Action: Spiritual Exploration Checklist*

Create a checklist of spiritual exploration activities that interest you both. Include diverse practices, places of worship to visit, and courses to consider. Set aside time each month to explore one item on the list, reflecting on what you learn and how it impacts your relationship.

Incorporating these activities into your relationship can foster a deeper understanding and appreciation of each other's spiritual paths. It's not about forcing each other into a specific mold but about celebrating and supporting each other's unique journeys. As you explore your spirituality together, you'll find that your relationship becomes richer and more fulfilling. Each new experience, whether it's a shared meditation session or a lively discussion over dinner, adds another layer to your connection. So, grab that checklist, step out of your comfort zone, and see where your curiosity leads. You might just discover that the journey is as rewarding as the destination.

## 6.3 RESPECTING INDIVIDUAL JOURNEYS: BALANCING PERSONAL AND SHARED GROWTH

Picture this: you've just discovered a new passion for early morning meditation, while your spouse finds solace in reading spiritual texts late at night. These individual pursuits are more than just hobbies; they're vital to your personal development and, ultimately, to your relationship's strength. Personal growth is like adding new ingredients to a favorite dish—it enhances the flavor, making both the meal and the relationship richer. Recognizing the value of these personal spiritual experiences can transform how you relate to one another. Each spouse's journey adds a unique dimension to your shared life, offering fresh perspectives and insights that can deepen your connection. Supporting each other's faith pursuits is like cheering from the sidelines, providing encouragement and space to explore and grow without pressure or judgment.

Balancing personal and shared growth requires a delicate dance, much like finding the rhythm on a crowded dance floor. It's about giving room for solo moves while ensuring there are moments to twirl together. Setting aside time for both personal and couple's spiritual practices is essential. You might dedicate a quiet hour in the morning to your meditation while reserving evenings for shared prayer or reflection. This balance respects each spouse's need for individual reflection while fostering shared spiritual moments that can enrich your bond. Encouraging personal reflection alongside joint activities ensures that both spouses feel valued and fulfilled. It's about weaving together threads of independent and shared experiences to create a tapestry that is both intricate and cohesive.

Supporting each other's journeys isn't just about providing space; it's about actively championing your spouse's growth. Celebrate personal spiritual milestones and achievements, whether it's completing a spiritual study or reaching a personal epiphany. These celebrations don't have to be grand—sometimes a simple acknowledgment or a shared toast can speak volumes. Offering encouragement during periods of doubt or challenge can be a lifeline. We all hit rough patches, and knowing that your spouse believes in you can make all the difference. It's like having a safety net while walking a tightrope, providing the assurance needed to take those daring steps toward growth.

To balance growth effectively, consider creating a spiritual growth plan that includes both individual and joint goals. This plan acts like a roadmap, guiding your personal and shared spiritual journeys without dictating the route. It can include individual goals, like reading a specific spiritual book, and joint goals, such as attending a retreat together. Reflective journaling alongside shared discussions can help track progress and provide insight into each other's growth. This practice allows you to document your thoughts and reflections, creating a tangible record of your spiritual evolution. It's like keeping a diary of your adventures, filled with lessons learned and memories cherished.

As you navigate the complexities of personal and shared growth, remember that each spouse's journey is a gift to the relationship. It's about appreciating the unique contributions each spouse brings, like mixing different colors on a palette to create a masterpiece. By embracing both the individual and shared aspects of your spiritual lives, you enrich your relationship, making it more vibrant and resilient. This balance allows you to grow together while respecting each other's individuality, ensuring that both spouses feel supported and valued. Whether you're meditating in silence or discussing a shared insight over dinner, these moments of growth add depth and richness to the tapestry of your relationship.

## 6.4 UNITY IN DIVERSITY: CELEBRATING DIFFERENT SPIRITUAL BACKGROUNDS

Ever notice how a potluck dinner is always more exciting when everyone brings their own dish? It's a feast of flavors where every contribution adds richness to the table. Similarly, when you and your spouse come from different spiritual backgrounds, your relationship becomes a vibrant tapestry woven from a multitude of threads. These varied backgrounds are not just differences to manage but treasures to explore. They bring unique perspectives and traditions into your relationship, enriching your shared life with a depth that might otherwise be missed. Imagine the joy of discovering a new tradition or spiritual practice through your spouse's eyes, each revelation offering a new lens through which to view the world.

Celebrating spiritual diversity isn't just about acknowledging these differences; it's about honoring them and finding ways to integrate them into your shared life. You might start by sharing and incorporating different cultural or religious traditions. Think of it as creating a mosaic with pieces from each of your backgrounds. Perhaps you celebrate Christmas with a blend of customs, adding a twist from your spouse's tradition that you never knew existed. Exploring the historical and spiritual roots of each spouse's faith can also be enlightening. It's like taking a journey through time, understanding where your spiritual beliefs come from and how they've shaped who you are today. These explorations can deepen your connection, offering insights into each other's values and dreams.

But how do you navigate these differences without stepping on each other's toes? One approach is to practice active acceptance and inclusivity. It's about embracing your spouse's beliefs and traditions, even if they're different from your own. This doesn't mean abandoning your own spiritual path but finding common ground in shared values and beliefs. It's like finding a melody in a duet, where each voice is distinct but harmonizes beautifully with the other. By focusing on what unites you rather than what divides you, you can create a relationship that thrives on both unity and diversity. It's about seeing each other's spiritual backgrounds as complementary rather than conflicting, creating a relationship that is both dynamic and cohesive.

Activities that celebrate diversity can further strengthen this unity. Hosting gatherings that celebrate cultural or religious festivals is a wonderful way to honor and embrace both backgrounds. Imagine a dinner party where each dish tells a story, offering a taste of your respective cultures and traditions. These gatherings become more than just meals; they're celebrations of the diversity that enriches your relationship. Another idea is to create a shared project that highlights elements from both backgrounds. This could be a scrapbook of meaningful traditions, a joint art project that reflects your shared spiritual journey, or even a series of photographs capturing moments of unity in diversity. These projects not only celebrate your unique backgrounds but also create a tangible reminder of the richness they bring to your relationship.

As you explore and celebrate your spiritual diversity, remember that these differences are not obstacles but opportunities. They invite you to step outside your comfort zone and embrace the beauty that comes from blending different traditions and perspectives. By celebrating the richness of your diverse backgrounds, you can create a relationship that is not only resilient but also deeply fulfilling. It's about finding joy in the journey of discovery, where each new insight adds another layer to the tapestry of your shared life. With open hearts and minds, you can navigate the complexities of spiritual diversity with grace and understanding, creating a relationship that is both grounded and expansive.

In the grand scheme of things, embracing spiritual diversity is just one piece of the puzzle. It's a reminder that love knows no bounds and that the beauty of a relationship lies in its ability to grow and evolve. As we move forward, we'll continue to explore how these principles can be applied to other aspects of your relationship, building a foundation that is both strong and adaptable.

# CHAPTER 7
## CREATING LASTING HABITS

Imagine your relationship as a beautiful garden. Sometimes it flourishes with vibrant blooms, and other times it might look like it could use a little TLC. One of the best ways to keep it blooming year-round is by establishing routines that nurture your spiritual and relational growth. Creating lasting habits is like having a trusted gardener—you know, the kind who knows exactly when to water and when to let the sun do its work. These routines not only provide structure but also foster stability and growth, much like a well-tended garden thrives in the right environment.

## 7.1 BUILDING A ROUTINE: ESTABLISHING DEVOTIONAL PRACTICES

Consistent devotional routines are like the daily watering and sunlight your relationship needs to thrive. They offer a rhythm that brings stability, much like how the sun rises and sets each day. Regular practices help solidify the foundation of your relationship, turning sporadic spiritual moments into a steady stream of nourishment. By setting a specific time each day for devotionals, you ensure that this vital connection becomes a non-negotiable part of your life. It might be a calm morning before the world wakes up, with coffee in hand and scripture in your lap, or an evening retreat where the day's blessings and challenges are reflected upon.

Establishing these routines begins with selecting devotional materials that resonate with both of you. Look for resources that align with your shared values and interests, something that sparks curiosity and conversation. Maybe it's a book of daily reflections that speaks to both your hearts or a podcast that provokes thought and dialogue. Once you've got the materials, create a comfortable and inspiring space for your devotional activities. This space doesn't have to be grand; it could be a cozy corner of your living room with a couple of comfy chairs and a favorite candle. The goal is to make it inviting, a place where both of you feel at ease and ready to connect with each other and with God.

The benefits of these routines extend beyond spiritual growth; they enhance your personal and relational well-being. Establishing a routine encourages discipline, turning your spiritual practices into habits that anchor your relationship. It's a commitment to each other and to your shared faith journey. Regular devotionals provide opportunities for reflection, offering a moment of pause in a busy day where you can reconnect, not just with each other, but with your shared values and goals. This reflection fosters a deeper understanding and connection, nurturing the intimacy that forms the bedrock of your relationship.

Take, for example, the simple practice of morning devotionals with coffee and prayer. It's a moment to start the day in unity, setting intentions and seeking guidance for whatever lies ahead. This routine becomes a touchstone, a reminder that you're both in this together, supported by a faith that guides and sustains you. Alternatively, evening reflections on the day's blessings and challenges can offer closure and peace. As you sit together and recount the day's events, you create a space for gratitude and growth, acknowledging the highs and learning from the lows. These practices turn the ordinary into the extraordinary, weaving spirituality into the fabric of your everyday life.

### *Reflection Section: Craft Your Devotional Space*

Take some time to discuss how you envision your devotional routine. What materials excite you? How can you make your environment more inviting? Consider jotting down your ideas and setting a date to create your sacred space together. This collaboration can make the practice more meaningful and tailored to both of your preferences.

Incorporating these routines into your daily life doesn't have to feel like a chore. Think of it as a gift you give to each other and to your relationship. It's about creating a rhythm that resonates with your unique dynamic, a melody that plays softly in the background, guiding your steps and strengthening your bond. With each devotional, you're not just nurturing your spiritual life; you're cultivating a relationship that thrives on connection, understanding, and love.

## 7.2 ACCOUNTABILITY SPOUSES: SUPPORTING EACH OTHER'S GROWTH

Imagine you and your spouse as a dynamic duo, not unlike Batman and Robin, each playing a crucial role in the other's growth. Accountability spouses in spiritual growth function much like that famous marriage, providing balance, support, and a gentle nudge when you might rather hit the snooze button. Regular check-ins and discussions on spiritual goals act as your Bat-Signal, illuminating the path you both want to pursue and ensuring you stay on track. These conversations don't need to be formal sit-downs. They can happen over dinner, during a walk, or whenever you both feel most open and connected. The key is to regularly touch base, sharing progress, challenges, and insights. This regular communication builds a strong foundation of mutual support, allowing both spouses to flourish in their spiritual journeys.

Being an effective accountability spouse involves a delicate balance of support and challenge. Think of it as being a personal coach who knows when to push for that extra rep and when to offer a comforting pat on the back. Setting mutual goals and tracking progress together is a great starting point. These goals should reflect both individual aspirations and shared objectives, creating a roadmap that guides your spiritual growth. Keep track of these goals, perhaps in a shared journal or a simple note on your fridge, as a reminder of your commitments. Constructive feedback is vital, too. It's not about criticism but about offering insights that help each other grow. Encourage each other with words that uplift and motivate. "I believe in you" goes a long way, turning potential road-blocks into stepping stones.

Shared accountability in relationships strengthens bonds in ways you might not anticipate. It builds trust and transparency through open communication, creating an environment where both spouses feel safe to express their true selves. When you know that your spouse is genuinely invested in your growth, it reinforces the commitment to personal and shared development. This mutual investment transforms challenges into opportunities for deeper understanding and connection. When both spouses actively participate in each other's spiritual growth, the relationship becomes a living testament to their shared values and faith. It's like building a house together, where every brick laid is a symbol of love and dedication.

There are many activities that can promote accountability within your relationship. Consider scheduling weekly goal-setting meetings. These gatherings are not about formality but about creating a space to discuss achievements, challenges, and next steps. They provide an opportunity to celebrate wins, no matter how small, and to strategize around obstacles. These meetings can be as simple as a ten-minute chat over coffee or a more structured discussion with notes and plans. Another way to encourage growth is by spousing in a spiritual course or workshop. Choose a topic that intrigues you both and dive in. This shared learning experience not only enhances your knowledge but also strengthens your bond as you explore new ideas together. It's like taking a mini-adventure, where every discovery is a shared victory.

Being accountability spouses means being each other's biggest cheerleaders, ready to support, challenge, and celebrate at a moment's notice. This relationship dynamic isn't just about keeping each other on track; it's about fostering a deep connection that supports growth in all its forms. By embracing this role, you create a marriage that nurtures both the individual and the collective, turning your relationship into a vibrant tapestry of shared goals and achievements.

## 7.3 REFLECTIVE PRACTICES: JOURNALING AND SELF-REFLECTION

Picture self-reflection as a cozy chat with your best friend—yourself. It's where you can be completely honest, no filters or pretenses. This kind of introspection is a powerhouse for personal growth. It boosts self-awareness, helping you understand why you react the way you do or why certain patterns keep popping up in your life. When you take time to reflect, you gain insights into your behavior and emotions, which can transform your relationship dynamics too. Reflective practices, especially journaling, allow you to document thoughts and feelings, offering an emotional release and a way to process complex emotions. Imagine it as a canvas where you paint your daily experiences with words. These practices are not just about penning down what happened but about exploring the why and how, diving into the depths of your experiences to uncover gems of wisdom.

Setting aside dedicated time each week for reflection might sound like another task on an already packed schedule, but think of it as a mini-vacation for your mind. It's a moment where you pause the hustle and bustle of life to tune into your inner world. During this time, guided journaling prompts can be a helpful tool. These prompts encourage you to explore specific topics, from examining a recent argument to dreaming about future goals. They act as a starting point, gently nudging you to dig deeper into your thoughts and feelings. Perhaps you start with a simple question like, "What am I grateful for today?" or "What did I learn from a challenging situation this week?" These prompts help you move beyond surface-level musings, guiding you toward meaningful self-discovery.

Journaling offers a plethora of benefits for both spiritual and emotional well-being. It's like clearing the fog from a window, allowing you to see your life with greater clarity and understanding. By writing down your experiences, you create a safe space for processing emotions, a sanctuary where no judgment exists. This process fosters growth, helping you recognize patterns and make informed decisions about how to move forward. Journaling also enhances your ability to articulate your thoughts, making it easier to communicate with others. When you understand yourself better, you're more equipped to share those insights with your spouse, fostering deeper intimacy and connection.

Reflective exercises are a great way to kick-start or deepen your journaling practice. One such exercise is writing gratitude lists. Focusing on the positives in your life shifts your perspective from what's lacking to what's abundant. It's like putting on a pair of rose-tinted glasses that highlight the beauty in everyday moments. Another exercise involves reflecting on spiritual teachings and their impact on your personal beliefs. Consider a passage or lesson that resonated with you recently and explore how it shapes your worldview. These reflections can lead to revelations about your values and how they influence your actions. They provide a foundation for personal growth, allowing you to align your life more closely with your beliefs and aspirations.

### *Interactive Element: Guided Journaling Prompts*

Try setting aside 15 minutes each week for journaling with these prompts: "What brought me joy this week?" "How did I handle a recent challenge?" "What is one thing I appreciate about myself?" Use these questions to guide your reflections, and notice how your understanding deepens over time.

The act of journaling transforms solitary reflection into a tangible form, a record of your journey that you can look back on. It becomes a mirror reflecting your inner world, capturing the nuances of your thoughts and emotions. As you engage in these reflective practices, you'll find that they not only enhance your self-awareness but also enrich your relationship with your spouse. With each entry, you're not just learning about yourself; you're building a bridge to more meaningful connections.

## 7.4 CELEBRATING MILESTONES: RECOGNIZING PROGRESS AND GROWTH

Picture this: You've just climbed to the top of a mountain, breathless, with your spouse by your side. You pause, take in the view, and celebrate the feat of reaching the summit together. In relationships, celebrating milestones can be just as exhilarating. Recognizing achievements, whether they're personal or shared, is like planting flags at the peaks of your journey. These celebrations aren't just about marking time; they're about acknowledging the growth and effort that brought you to this point. Whether it's completing a shared spiritual goal, navigating a challenging season, or simply sticking together through thick and thin, each milestone is a testament to your commitment and growth.

Celebrating achievements can take many forms, from the grand to the understated. Planning special outings or events is a wonderful way to commemorate these moments. Imagine whisking your spouse away for a weekend getaway to celebrate an anniversary of overcoming a significant challenge. Alternatively, a quiet dinner at home, complete with your favorite meal and shared memories, can be equally meaningful. For those who enjoy a creative touch, consider creating visual displays of your milestones. A timeline or scrapbook filled with photos, mementos, and notes can serve as a beautiful reminder of how far you've come. These visual representations not only celebrate your achievements but also provide a tangible source of inspiration when the going gets tough.

Celebrations have a profound impact on relationships by reinforcing mutual support and encouragement. They're like the exclamation marks in your love story, highlighting the moments that deserve to be remembered. By acknowledging each other's accomplishments, you build a sense of pride and fulfillment in your shared journey. Celebrating milestones reminds you both of the strength and resilience that have carried you through challenges. It's a chance to pause and reflect on the journey, appreciating the growth and learning that have occurred along the way. This reflection fosters a deeper connection, reminding you of the love and support that are the foundation of your relationship.

Let's explore some examples of meaningful celebrations. Hosting a dinner to share successes with friends or family can be a delightful way to mark a milestone. Imagine gathering your loved ones around the table, sharing stories and laughter as you celebrate your achievement. It's an opportunity to not only honor the milestone but also to express gratitude for the support of those around you. Another meaningful celebration could involve engaging in a reflective activity to honor growth. Consider creating a vision board that encapsulates your shared goals and dreams. This visual representation serves as a powerful reminder of your aspirations, inspiring you to continue reaching for new heights together. As you piece together images and words, you create a shared vision that reinforces your commitment to each other and to the future you're building together.

Celebrating milestones is an integral part of nurturing a healthy, vibrant relationship. It's about acknowledging the hard work, dedication, and love that have brought you to where you are today. These celebrations infuse your relationship with joy and gratitude, creating a reservoir of positive memories that you can draw upon during challenging times. As you continue to navigate the peaks and valleys of your relationship, remember that each milestone, no matter how small, is worth celebrating. These moments of recognition and reflection not only honor your past achievements but also inspire your future endeavors. Whether it's a grand celebration or a quiet moment of reflection, take the time to acknowledge the progress and growth that define your love story.

# CHAPTER 8
## ADDRESSING COMMON CHALLENGES

Have you ever felt like your relationship is a juggling act, balancing flaming torches while riding a unicycle? Between work deadlines, soccer practice, and trying to remember if you fed the cat, it's no wonder relationships can feel like they're getting the short end of the stick. This chapter is about tackling the common challenges that come with the territory, starting with time management—a skill that seems as elusive as finding unicorns in your backyard.

## 8.1 TIME MANAGEMENT: PRIORITIZING YOUR RELATIONSHIP AMIDST BUSY SCHEDULES

In today's fast-paced world, busyness is worn like a badge of honor. It's as if saying "I'm so busy" has replaced "How are you?" as the standard greeting. But all this hustle and bustle can wreak havoc on relationships. When you're constantly on the go, balancing work, family, and personal commitments, your relationship can start to feel like that plant you keep forgetting to water—parched and wilting. The impact of a hectic lifestyle is undeniable. It can lead to feelings of isolation and neglect, leaving couples feeling like ships passing in the night, or worse, like strangers living parallel lives under the same roof.

Signs of relationship neglect can be subtle yet telling. Maybe you find yourself forgetting important dates, like anniversaries or birthdays, or you feel disconnected, even when you're sitting right next to each other. Perhaps conversations have become quick exchanges about logistics rather than meaningful dialogues about hopes and dreams. These signs are like the red flags on a beach warning of strong currents—they're easy to overlook until you're swept away. Recognizing these signs is the first step in re-prioritizing your relationship amidst the chaos.

Effective time management can be a game-changer for couples looking to prioritize their relationship. One strategy is creating a shared calendar to manage activities. This is not just about scheduling dentist appointments or kids' playdates; it's about intentionally blocking out time for each other. Think of it as planting flags for date nights, weekend getaways, or even just a quiet evening at home. Setting boundaries is another crucial step. It's about protecting your personal time together like a precious artifact. This might mean saying no to extra work assignments or social obligations that encroach on your relationship time. It's about creating a sacred space that nurtures your bond, allowing it to flourish.

The benefits of prioritizing relationship time are profound. Regular connection enhances communication and intimacy, allowing you to engage in meaningful conversations rather than superficial exchanges. This dedicated time fosters a supportive environment, reducing stress and reinforcing the idea that you're a team facing life together. It's like building a fortress around your relationship, ensuring it withstands the pressures of daily life. When you make time for each other, you're not just strengthening your bond; you're also investing in your future, creating a solid foundation that supports both spouses' growth and happiness.

Practical time management techniques can help you carve out this crucial time. Time-blocking can be an effective method for ensuring relationship-focused activities don't get lost in the shuffle. By setting aside specific blocks of time for each other, you're making a commitment that says, "You're important to me." Another useful technique is implementing a weekly check-in. This isn't just about syncing schedules; it's about planning and scheduling together, discussing the week ahead, and ensuring that you're aligned in your priorities and goals. It's like a mini board meeting for your relationship, ensuring everything is on track and both spouses feel valued and heard.

### *Interactive Element: Weekly Relationship Check-in Template*

Consider setting aside time each week for a relationship check-in. Use this template to guide your conversation:

1. **Review the past week:** What were the highlights and challenges?
2. **Plan for the upcoming week:** What activities or events are on the horizon?
3. **Set intentions:** What do you hope to achieve together this week?
4. **Discuss any concerns:** Are there any unresolved issues or worries?

By using this template, you can facilitate open communication and ensure that you're both on the same page, fostering a stronger, more connected relationship.

Time management in relationships is about more than just finding time; it's about making time. It's about prioritizing what truly matters and creating a life where your relationship isn't just surviving but thriving. So, the next time you feel overwhelmed by the demands of everyday life, remember that your relationship deserves the same attention and care as any other important commitment. After all, love, like any good plant, flourishes when it's nurtured.

## 8.2 OVERCOMING ROUTINE FATIGUE: KEEPING DEVOTIONALS ENGAGING

Picture this: it's a quiet morning, and you and your spouse sit down for your daily devotional. But instead of feeling inspired, you find yourselves going through the motions, like two actors stuck in a play they've performed a million times. Routine fatigue has crept in, turning what was once a sacred time into a mundane ritual. Losing enthusiasm for devotional activities is a common experience. You might start to feel like you're just checking a box, rather than connecting with each other and your faith. Repetitiveness can make devotionals feel stale, leading to a struggle to find meaning in the exercises that once brought you closer together. It's like eating the same meal every day—eventually, even your favorite dish loses its flavor.

So, how do you shake things up and breathe new life into your devotional practice? Introducing new formats or materials can be a game-changer. Think of it as adding a sprinkle of spice to a familiar recipe. Instead of sticking to the same old routine, explore different devotional guides or resources. You might try a new book of reflections or online resources that offer fresh perspectives. Variety keeps things interesting and prevents monotony from setting in. Another way to revitalize your practice is by incorporating multimedia elements, like podcasts or videos. These can provide a different angle on familiar topics, offering insights that resonate in new ways. Imagine listening to a podcast episode that sparks a lively discussion or watching a video that inspires you both to think differently about a scripture passage.

Creativity plays a crucial role in maintaining engagement with devotionals. By infusing art or music into your sessions, you can transform them into something vibrant and dynamic. Maybe you start each devotional with a piece of music that sets the tone, or you incorporate painting or drawing as a form of reflection. Encouraging personal interpretation and expression of scripture can also enhance your experience. Rather than sticking strictly to a prescribed format, allow yourselves the freedom to explore how the scriptures speak to you personally. It's about making the practice your own, turning it into a canvas where you both paint your spiritual journey.

Consider organizing themed devotionals focused on specific topics. One week, you might explore the theme of gratitude, reflecting on different passages that highlight thankfulness. The next, you could delve into forgiveness, discussing how it applies to your lives. This thematic approach adds depth and focus, allowing you to explore the richness of your faith from various angles. Experimenting with different settings or environments can also add a new dimension to your practice. Instead of always gathering in the same spot, try taking your devotional outdoors, to a park or even your backyard.

The change in scenery can provide a fresh perspective, turning what was once routine into an adventure.

***Reflection Section: Explore Your Devotional Creativity***

Take some time to reflect on how you can infuse creativity into your devotional practice. Consider what elements resonate with you—whether it's music, art, or themed sessions—and jot down ideas for incorporating them into your routine. Challenge yourselves to try something new each week and see how it transforms your experience.

By embracing these strategies, you can overcome routine fatigue and keep your devotionals engaging. It's about rediscovering the joy and meaning that brought you together in the first place, turning each session into a source of inspiration and connection. Devotionals are more than a task to complete—they are an opportunity to deepen your bond, explore your faith, and create moments of beauty and reflection amidst the busyness of life. As you explore these new possibilities, you may find that your devotional time becomes not just a habit but a cherished part of your shared spiritual journey.

## 8.3 APPLYING SCRIPTURE: MAKING BIBLICAL LESSONS RELEVANT TO DAILY LIFE

Think about how often you find yourself scrolling through social media, bombarded by a whirlwind of modern challenges, from managing work stress to navigating complicated relationships. You might wonder how ancient texts, written in a time of sandals and scrolls, can offer guidance in today's fast-paced, tech-driven world. Yet, bridging the gap between the Bible's timeless wisdom and today's contemporary issues is not only possible but incredibly enriching. The key lies in finding personal relevance in scripture for everyday situations. When you read the Bible, you're not just engaging with history; you're accessing a treasure trove of insights that can illuminate your path and help you tackle modern dilemmas with grace and wisdom.

To make these ancient teachings applicable to your life, consider using reflective questions to connect scripture to personal experiences. Imagine approaching a Bible verse with the curiosity of a detective, asking probing questions like, "How does this apply to my current situation?" or "What can I learn from this to improve my relationships?" These questions act as bridges, linking the past and present, allowing the wisdom of scripture to speak directly to your heart. Another practical method is developing action plans based on scriptural insights. It's one thing to nod along to a sermon, but it's another to take those insights and turn them into actionable steps. For example, if you read about forgiveness, you might decide to reach out to someone you've been avoiding. Creating an action plan helps transform passive reading into active living, making biblical lessons a tangible part of your daily routine.

The benefits of applying scripture to daily life are as vast as they are profound. Biblical lessons can guide decision-making by enhancing your moral and ethical understanding in various contexts. Whether you're grappling with a tough choice at work or a personal dilemma, scripture offers a moral compass, helping you navigate with integrity and compassion. Moreover, scripture provides comfort and guidance during difficult times. Life's storms are inevitable, but the Bible offers a refuge, a place to find peace and reassurance amidst chaos. It's like having a wise friend who knows exactly what to say to calm your fears and offer perspective.

Consider this: you're facing a tricky situation at work, perhaps a conflict with a colleague. Instead of resorting to office politics or gossip, you could turn to biblical stories for guidance. The story of David and Goliath, for instance, might inspire you to face your challenges with courage and faith, while the wisdom of Solomon could offer insights into resolving disputes with fairness and wisdom. By integrating these stories into your approach, you gain new perspectives and strategies to handle workplace challenges gracefully. Similarly, applying proverbs to your interpersonal relationships can be transformative. Proverbs often contain nuggets of wisdom that speak to the heart of human behavior, encouraging patience, humility, and understanding. Imagine using these proverbs as guiding principles in your interactions, fostering healthier, more meaningful connections with those around you.

### *Reflection Section: Connecting Scripture with Life*

Take a moment to reflect on a current challenge you're facing. Choose a scripture that resonates with you and ask yourself: How does this apply to my situation? What action steps can I take based on its teachings? Write down your thoughts and revisit them as you navigate your challenge.

Incorporating scripture into your daily life is about more than just reading; it's about living those teachings in practical, meaningful ways. It's about allowing the wisdom of the Bible to shape your actions, decisions, and relationships, turning ancient lessons into modern-day guides. As you engage with scripture, you'll find that it offers not just answers but also the strength and inspiration to face life's challenges with faith and resilience.

## 8.4 NAVIGATING LIFE CHANGES: ADAPTING YOUR RELATIONSHIP STRATEGIES

Life is a series of transitions, isn't it? Just when you think you've got everything under control, something shifts, and you find yourself on a new path. These changes can come in many forms. Picture this: you've just snagged a promotion at work, which is fantastic, but it also means longer hours and maybe even relocating to a new city. Or perhaps you're welcoming a new member to your family, which is both exhilarating and exhausting. Let's not forget about the times when you have to step into a caregiver role for aging parents. Each of these scenarios presents unique challenges and opportunities for growth in your relationship. They can feel like juggling flaming torches while riding a unicycle, but with the right mindset and strategies, you can navigate them with grace and confidence.

Adapting to such life changes requires a solid foundation of communication. It's like building a bridge over turbulent waters. Without open and honest dialogue, you risk drifting apart amidst the chaos. Establishing open lines of communication is crucial. This means creating a safe space where both spouses can express their fears, hopes, and expectations. Whether it's a late-night chat over a cup of tea or a weekend walk in the park, these conversations are the lifeline that keeps you connected. It's about being vulnerable and honest, sharing your thoughts without fear of judgment. This openness can help you both feel heard and understood, strengthening your bond.

Setting new goals that reflect evolving circumstances is another key strategy. Life changes often require a shift in priorities, and it's important to ensure that you're both on the same page. Maybe your career goals need adjusting, or perhaps you want to focus more on family time. Whatever the change, having a clear set of shared goals can provide direction and purpose. Think of it as recalibrating your compass, ensuring that you're both heading in the same direction. These goals serve as a roadmap, guiding you through the twists and turns of life with a shared sense of purpose and intention.

The benefits of adaptability in relationships are as rewarding as they are transformative. By embracing flexibility, you strengthen your resilience and unity during challenging times. It's like standing side by side in a storm, knowing that you have each other's back. This adaptability encourages growth and innovation within the relationship, opening the door to new experiences and adventures. It's about seeing change not as a threat but as an opportunity to learn and grow together. By staying open and adaptable, you create a dynamic marriage that thrives on change, using it as a catalyst for deeper connection and understanding.

To support each other through these transitions, consider engaging in exercises designed to foster adaptability. Creating a shared vision board for the future can be a powerful tool. Gather images, quotes, and symbols that reflect your shared dreams and aspirations, and arrange them on a board. This visual representation serves as a constant reminder of what you're working towards, keeping you both motivated and focused. Regular check-ins are also essential for assessing and adjusting strategies. Set aside time to discuss what's working and what's not, making adjustments as needed. These sessions are like tune-ups for your relationship, ensuring that you're both aligned and moving forward together.

Navigating life changes is no small feat, but with open communication, shared goals, and a willingness to adapt, you can turn these challenges into opportunities for growth. Life is full of surprises, but with the right strategies in place, you can face them together with strength and resilience. As you embrace these changes, remember that each transition is a chance to deepen your connection and build a relationship that's as dynamic as it is enduring.

# CHAPTER 9
# COMMUNITY AND SUPPORT

I magine for a moment that you're a lone cowboy, riding through the Wild West, but instead of tumbleweeds and saloons, you're navigating the modern landscape of life's challenges. Now, while it might sound romantic to go it alone—just you, your horse, and the open road—let's be honest: life is a lot more manageable when you have a posse riding alongside you. This is where the concept of community, particularly life groups, comes into play. Life groups are like your band of trusty sidekicks, offering support, camaraderie, and plenty of laughs along the way. They're the people who help you navigate the ups and downs, providing a sense of belonging and shared purpose that can make even the toughest trails feel conquerable.

Life groups play a crucial role in spiritual growth by providing a supportive environment for couples. These groups are like a warm blanket on a cold day, wrapping you in a sense of security and comfort as you explore your spiritual journey. They foster a sense of belonging that can be hard to find in today's fast-paced world.

When you're part of a life group, you're not just attending a meeting; you're becoming part of a community where everyone is committed to growing together. This shared purpose creates a safe space for discussing spiritual and relational challenges. Whether you're wrestling with a big question about faith or struggling with a personal issue, a life group offers a sanctuary where you can share your struggles and receive support from others who are on a similar path.

The benefits of participating in life groups are as diverse as the members themselves. First and foremost, life groups are fertile ground for building lasting friendships rooted in faith. These aren't just casual acquaintances; they're the kind of friendships that stand the test of time. Heidi's parents, for example, have been part of a small group for over 25 years, illustrating the potential for deep, long-lasting connections that enrich your life in countless ways. Additionally, life groups offer the opportunity to gain diverse perspectives on spiritual teachings. When you bring people from different backgrounds and experiences together, you open the door to new insights and understandings that can deepen your own faith. It's like attending a potluck dinner, where everyone brings a dish, and you leave with a full plate and a happy heart.

Finding the right life group can feel a bit like dating. You might have to try a few before you find the perfect fit, but the effort is well worth it. Consider the size of the group and the frequency of meetings. Some prefer the intimacy of a smaller group that meets weekly, while others might enjoy the energy of a larger group that gathers monthly. Think about what works best for you and your spouse's schedule. It's also important to evaluate the group's focus and alignment with your personal beliefs. Are you looking for a group that dives deep into Bible study, or one that focuses more on fellowship and social activities? Understanding what you're seeking will help you find a group that feels like home.

Life groups are dynamic and offer a variety of activities that enhance connection and growth. Group Bible studies and discussions are a staple, providing a structured way to explore scripture and share insights. These sessions are often lively, sparking engaging conversations that challenge and inspire. Beyond study, many groups participate in community service projects, allowing members to live out their faith in tangible ways. Whether it's organizing a food drive, volunteering at a local shelter, or participating in a neighborhood cleanup, these activities strengthen the bonds within the group and serve the broader community. It's a powerful way to put faith into action, turning beliefs into deeds that make a difference.

### *Reflection Section: Finding Your Perfect Fit*

Consider what you're looking for in a life group. What activities and focus align with your values and interests? Reflect on your needs and jot down a few key criteria. Use this as a guide when exploring different groups to help you find one that feels like a perfect fit.

Life groups are there to offer support, encouragement, and a sense of belonging. They're the community that celebrates with you in times of joy and stands beside you in times of struggle. When you find the right group, it's like discovering a second family—one that nurtures your spirit and enriches your life in ways you never imagined.

## 9.1 MENTORSHIP: LEARNING FROM OTHER COUPLES' JOURNEYS

In life, it's often said that experience is the best teacher, but sometimes it's even better to learn from someone else's experiences—preferably without making the same mistakes. That's where the beauty of mentorship comes into play, especially in relationships. Picture this: you're facing a tricky situation in your marriage, perhaps a disagreement that just won't resolve, like a stubborn stain on your favorite shirt. Now imagine having a wise couple, seasoned by years of marriage, who can offer you guidance and advice. These mentors become like a lighthouse, guiding you through the fog of relational challenges with their beacon of experience and insight.

Mentorship offers a treasure trove of benefits that can positively impact your relationship. When you engage with a mentor couple, you gain new skills and perspectives on relationship dynamics. It's like having a personal coach who can help you navigate the tricky waters of marriage, offering tools and techniques that have stood the test of time. These seasoned spouses have likely encountered similar challenges and can provide strategies that worked for them. They offer a fresh perspective, helping you see your relationship from a different angle and find solutions you might not have considered. Moreover, mentorship helps build a supportive network of mentors and peers. This network becomes a safe space where you can share your struggles, celebrate your victories, and receive encouragement. It's like joining a club where everyone is rooting for your success, cheering you on as you grow and thrive.

Finding the right mentor couple can feel a bit like searching for the perfect pair of shoes—they need to fit just right. Start by identifying couples who share your values and experiences. Maybe you've noticed a couple in your community or church who seem to have the kind of relationship you aspire to. They might be the ones who hold hands during long sermons or seem to have an unspoken language of love. Approach them with curiosity and openness, expressing your desire to learn from their experiences. Consider the mentor's availability and willingness to engage. A mentor relationship should be mutually beneficial, with both parties committed to sharing and growing together. Ensure that they have the time and willingness to invest in the relationship, as this commitment is key to a successful mentorship.

Once you've found a suitable mentor couple, there are numerous ways to engage with them. Regular meetings to discuss specific relationship topics can be incredibly valuable. These meetings might take place over a cup of coffee or during a leisurely walk in the park. Use this time to share your challenges, seek advice, and explore new ways to strengthen your relationship. It's an opportunity to dive deep into the intricacies of marriage, guided by those who have walked the path before you. Another effective way to engage with a mentor couple is through joint participation in faith-based activities or workshops. Attending a marriage retreat or a spiritual seminar together can create a shared experience that fosters growth and connection. These activities provide a platform for learning and reflection, allowing you to explore new dimensions of your relationship in a supportive environment.

Mentorship is about creating a marriage that enriches both your relationship and your mentors'. It's about learning from those who have traveled the road before you, absorbing their wisdom, and applying it to your own life. As you cultivate this mentor relationship, you'll find that it becomes a source of strength and inspiration, helping you navigate the complexities of marriage with grace and confidence.

## 9.2 SERVING TOGETHER: STRENGTHENING BONDS THROUGH SHARED PURPOSE

Have you ever noticed how a simple activity like cooking dinner together can turn into a full-blown comedy show, complete with burnt toast and the ever-popular "where did I put the spatula?" Serving together, especially in volunteer projects, has a similar effect but on a much grander scale. It's like turning your relationship into a dynamic duo, with matching capes and all. When couples engage in joint service projects, something magical happens. You build teamwork and cooperation by tackling shared tasks, like a well-oiled machine that sometimes sputters but always gets the job done. It's in these moments of shared purpose that you discover new depths of empathy and compassion, not only towards those you're helping but also towards each other. As you work side by side, whether hammering nails or ladling soup, you see firsthand how your combined efforts can make a tangible difference.

The impact of serving together extends far beyond the immediate project at hand. It strengthens the sense of purpose and unity within your relationship, creating a bond that's as solid as a well-built brick wall. There's something profoundly satisfying about knowing you're working together for a cause greater than yourselves. It's like planting seeds of kindness and watching them grow into a garden of shared memories and experiences. These moments become the stories you tell for years to come, the ones that start with "remember when we..." and end with laughter and a renewed sense of connection. Serving together also provides a unique opportunity to step outside your comfort zone and gain new perspectives. You'll meet people from all walks of life, each with their own stories and challenges, and these encounters can deepen your understanding of the world and your place within it.

If you're looking to strengthen your bond through service, there are plenty of meaningful volunteer activities to consider. Participating in local charity events or fundraisers is a great place to start. Whether it's organizing a charity run, hosting a bake sale for a good cause, or helping out at a fundraising gala, these events offer a chance to contribute your time and talents to something bigger. They're like social gatherings with a purpose, combining the fun of community events with the satisfaction of making a difference. For a more hands-on experience, consider volunteering at food banks or shelters. These organizations often rely on volunteers to help sort donations, prepare meals, or distribute supplies. Working together in these settings allows you to see the immediate impact of your efforts and feel the gratitude of those you're helping. It's a humbling experience that can bring you closer together as you reflect on the blessings in your own life.

There are also specific organizations and types of service that offer structured opportunities to serve together. Habitat for Humanity, for instance, organizes builds where volunteers work together to construct homes for families in need. Imagine the sense of accom-plishment in knowing that your teamwork helped put a roof over someone's head. It's like being part of a real-life fairy tale, where the happily-ever-after involves a solid house and a grateful family. Another option is participating in church-organized mission trips. These trips often combine service with travel, allowing you to immerse yourselves in new cultures while contributing to mean-ingful projects. Whether it's building schools, providing medical care, or supporting local communities, mission trips offer a unique blend of adventure and service. They're like a two-for-one deal, where you get to explore the world while making it a better place.

The act of serving together is a powerful way to enrich your relationship. It's about stepping into the world hand in hand, ready to face challenges and celebrate victories together. As you engage in these activities, you'll find that the shared sense of purpose and the memories you create become the foundation of a stronger, more connected marriage. The laughter, the teamwork, and the shared experiences all combine to create a tapestry of love and service that weaves through every aspect of your relationship.

## 9.3 FAITH WORKSHOPS: DEEPENING UNDERSTANDING THROUGH GROUP LEARNING

Imagine walking into a room filled with people, each carrying their own unique spiritual questions and insights, ready to embark on a shared exploration of faith. Faith workshops are like those moments when you discover a new book series that pulls you in and leaves you wanting more. They offer an opportunity to dive deep into specific spiritual topics, providing an in-depth exploration that can be hard to find in everyday life. These workshops are more than just a lecture; they're a platform for interactive learning and discussion, where you can engage with the material and with others in meaningful ways. Picture it as a lively exchange of ideas, where each question sparks a new insight and each discussion adds a layer to your understanding of faith.

The benefits of attending faith workshops are manifold. For starters, they offer a chance to gain new insights and understanding of faith that can enrich your spiritual journey. It's like adding tools to your spiritual toolbox, each one uniquely suited to help you navigate different aspects of your faith. Workshops can illuminate areas of your spiritual life that you've been curious about or struggling with, offering fresh perspectives and practical applications. Beyond the personal growth, these workshops also provide an opportunity to connect with like-minded individuals and build a sense of community. You're not just learning in isolation; you're part of a group that shares your interests and values, creating bonds that can last long after the workshop ends. It's like finding your tribe, a group of people who cheer you on and walk alongside you as you grow in faith.

Selecting the right workshop can feel a bit like choosing a film from the endless options on a streaming service. It's important to consider the workshop's focus and how it aligns with your personal interests and spiritual needs. Are you looking to deepen your understanding of prayer, explore the intersection of faith and science, or learn how to apply biblical teachings to your daily life? Whatever your interest, there's likely a workshop that speaks to that curiosity. Evaluate the credentials and reputation of the facilitators as well. A knowledgeable and engaging facilitator can make all the difference, turning a good workshop into a transformative experience. Look for facilitators who not only have expertise in the subject matter but also possess the ability to connect with participants on a personal level, creating an atmosphere of openness and trust.

Faith workshops come in a variety of topics and formats, each offering unique opportunities for growth and exploration. Retreat-style workshops focusing on prayer and meditation provide a serene environment where you can step away from the hustle and bustle of daily life and immerse yourself in spiritual reflection. These retreats often take place in beautiful, tranquil settings that invite contemplation and renewal. Imagine spending a weekend in the mountains, surrounded by nature, as you explore different forms of prayer and meditation, guided by experienced practitioners. It's a chance to unplug, recharge, and connect with the divine in a deeply personal way.

Interactive seminars on applying faith in daily life are another popular format. These workshops focus on practical applications of spiritual teachings, offering strategies for integrating faith into every aspect of your life. You might learn how to bring your faith into your workplace, navigate relationships through a spiritual lens, or use biblical principles to guide your decision-making. The interactive nature of these seminars encourages participation and dialogue, allowing you to share your experiences and learn from others. It's like a spiritual boot camp, where you leave with actionable steps and the motivation to apply what you've learned in your everyday life.

Faith workshops are a powerful way to deepen your understanding and connection to your spiritual beliefs. They offer a space for exploration, learning, and connection, providing a wealth of opportunities to grow in faith. As you consider attending a workshop, think about what you hope to gain and how it aligns with your spiritual goals. Whether you're looking to explore new topics, connect with others, or find practical applications for your faith, there's a workshop out there that can help you on your path.

# CHAPTER 10
## SUSTAINING A CHRIST-CENTERED RELATIONSHIP

Imagine navigating life like a road trip. You have the snacks packed, playlist ready, and the love of your life in the passenger seat. But without a map, even the best road trips can turn into scenic detours that test your patience and bladder capacity. In relationships, faith acts as that trusty map, guiding you through detours and ensuring you stay on course. When setting relationship goals, faith serves as the foundation, much like a GPS that recalibrates when you take an unexpected turn. Aligning your goals with biblical teachings and values ensures that your aspirations are not only ambitious but also anchored in a shared moral compass. This alignment fosters a sense of purpose and direction, transforming your relationship from a mere journey into a purposeful expedition.

Integrating faith into goal-setting is like weaving a golden thread through the fabric of your relationship. It starts with prayer, a quiet conversation with God that offers clarity and direction. Before setting goals, take a moment to pray together, asking for guidance and wisdom. This practice centers your intentions and invites divine insight into your decision-making processes. Using scripture as a framework for goal evaluation is equally important. Consider scripture as a checklist against which you measure your objectives. Does your goal align with biblical principles like love, patience, or kindness? This reflection ensures that your goals support a Christ-centered relationship, enhancing your bond through shared values.

Faith-based goals offer profound benefits, turning aspirations into a shared commitment that strengthens your relationship. They create a roadmap that keeps you aligned with each other and your spiritual beliefs. This alignment fosters a more profound sense of purpose, guiding you through life's challenges with confidence and grace. As you work towards these goals, you'll find that they strengthen your commitment to shared visions, transforming dreams into actionable steps. Setting and achieving these goals together reinforces your bond, making it more resilient and fulfilling. It's like planting seeds in a garden that, with time and care, blossoms into a vibrant testament to your shared faith and commitment.

### *Practical Exercise: Crafting a Faith-Based Mission Statement*

Try creating a faith-based mission statement for your relationship. Sit down together and discuss your core values and shared aspirations. What principles do you want to guide your relationship? Write these down, crafting a statement that encapsulates your shared vision. This mission statement is a constant reminder of your commitment to each other and a Christ-centered life. Revisit it regularly, holding goal-setting meetings with prayer and reflection to ensure your path remains aligned with your faith and love.

Incorporating faith into your relationship goals strengthens your bond and enriches your journey. It provides the guidance and support needed to navigate life's challenges, turning aspirations into a shared commitment that inspires and uplifts. As you continue to set and achieve these goals, you'll find that your relationship becomes a living testament to the power of faith and love.

## 10.1 SUSTAINING FAITH: KEEPING THE FLAME ALIVE

Maintaining spiritual fervor in a relationship can sometimes feel like trying to keep a campfire going during a downpour. Spiritual fatigue or burnout sneaks up like a cat in the night. One minute, you're praying and feeling connected; the next, you're questioning everything, wondering if your prayers are bouncing off the ceiling. Doubts can creep in, especially when life throws curveballs. It's natural to question your faith during challenging times or when you're caught in the monotony of routine. This is where many couples find themselves stuck, struggling to reignite the spiritual spark that once burned brightly. Recognizing these moments not as failures but as opportunities to grow stronger together is essential.

To rejuvenate your faith, consider shaking things up a bit. Engage in regular spiritual retreats or getaways. These don't need to be extravagant; a quiet weekend away from the hustle and bustle can work wonders. It's about stepping away from the everyday noise and finding solace in reflection and prayer. New worship or spiritual expression forms can also breathe new life into your spiritual practices. Try attending a different church service or exploring worship styles from other cultures. You might find that a fresh perspective helps you connect more deeply with your faith.

Community plays a crucial role in sustaining faith. Think of it as having a group of cheerleaders always ready to lift you. Participating in church activities and faith groups offers support and encouragement. Knowing you're not alone in your struggles and joys is comforting. Building relationships with other faith-driven couples can provide a network of support and accountability. Shared experiences and insights can be incredibly enriching, offering perspectives you might not have considered. It's like having a spiritual potluck where everyone brings something unique.

Practical activities can help nurture and sustain your faith. Establish a daily gratitude practice focused on faith. Each day, take a moment to reflect on the blessings and divine interventions you've experienced. This simple act can shift your perspective, highlighting the positive and reinforcing your spiritual connection. Creating a spiritual growth journal is another effective way to track progress and insights. Documenting your thoughts, prayers, and reflections lets you see how far you've come and where you want to go. It's a tangible reminder of your journey, encouraging you to stay committed to nurturing your faith.

## 10.2 CELEBRATING BLESSINGS: RECOGNIZING GOD'S HAND IN YOUR RELATIONSHIP

Think of gratitude as the gentle rain that nourishes the garden of your relationship, helping it flourish. Recognizing divine blessings is like acknowledging the moments when the sun breaks through the clouds, casting everything in a warm, golden glow. When you pause to see how divine intervention has played a part in your relationship's successes, you strengthen your faith and connection. Celebrating monumental or seemingly minor blessings keeps you attuned to the myriad ways God's presence enriches your lives. It's about noticing the everyday miracles, like a shared smile or an unexpected kindness, that transform ordinary days into extraordinary ones. Celebrating small and large joys creates a tapestry of gratitude that enhances your spiritual and relational dynamics.

Creating a shared blessings journal is one way to keep track of these blessings. Each of you can jot down moments where you've felt God's hand guiding you or when you've experienced unexpected joy. This journal becomes a testament to the divine acts that unfold in your lives, a chronicle of gratitude you can revisit whenever you need a reminder of how blessed you are. Hosting a gratitude dinner is another beautiful way to celebrate significant milestones. Gather loved ones around the table, share stories of gratitude, and acknowledge the divine presence that has brought you to where you are. These dinners don't have to be elaborate affairs; the focus is on the heart, not the menu. It's about coming together to give thanks and reflect on your journey and the blessings you've encountered.

Gratitude has a profound impact on spiritual growth. It's like a lens that shifts your perspective, helping you focus on the positive and fostering a hopeful outlook on life. When you consistently acknowledge and appreciate the blessings in your life, you develop a deeper trust in divine providence. This trust becomes a wellspring of strength, providing you with the peace and assurance needed to navigate life's challenges. It enhances your relationship by creating a foundation of positivity, turning everyday interactions into opportunities for connection and joy. As you cultivate gratitude, you'll find that it transforms your relationship, making it richer and more fulfilling.

Consider creating a visual gratitude board adorned with photos, scriptures, and symbols of the blessings you've experienced. This board is a constant reminder of God's presence in your lives, inspiring you to continue seeking and acknowledging the divine in the everyday. You might also organize a yearly retreat to reflect on and celebrate the blessings you've experienced over the past year. This retreat could be a simple day spent in nature or a weekend getaway to a peaceful location. The focus is reflection and gratitude, taking time to honor your shared journey and the blessings gracing your path.

## 10.3 THE JOURNEY AHEAD: EMBRACING ONGOING GROWTH

Picture your relationship like a garden. Sure, you've planted and watched the seeds bloom, but gardens aren't a one-and-done deal. They need constant care—pruning, watering, and talking to the plants when no one's watching. Relationships thrive on the same kind of ongoing attention, especially regarding spiritual growth. Embracing change and challenges becomes part of this dynamic. They aren't hurdles to avoid but growth opportunities. Think of it as the universe saying, "Hey, here's a chance to learn something new!" Encouraging lifelong learning in faith isn't just a nice idea; it's a necessity. It keeps you curious, flexible, and open to the wonders of what's to come. By diving into spiritual exploration, you're not just maintaining your relationship—you're enriching it, turning the ordinary into something extraordinary.

Setting regular growth goals is like setting destinations on your GPS. They give you direction and purpose, ensuring you're not just wandering. Regularly review these goals together. Ask yourselves, "How are we doing? What can we improve?" This isn't about nitpicking or pointing fingers; it's about supporting each other in something more significant. Engaging in new spiritual practices keeps things fresh. Maybe it's trying out meditation or starting a gratitude journal. Whatever it is, it should challenge you and push your boundaries. This exploration deepens your faith and strengthens your bond, making it more adaptable and resilient. Adopting a growth mindset transforms your relationship. It makes tackling change less daunting and more exciting. Resilience becomes second nature, like a muscle you've trained to flex when needed. It's the kind of adaptability that helps you weather any storm, turning potential roadblocks into stepping stones.

Consider practical exercises to keep the momentum going. Workshops or courses on spiritual topics can be enlightening. They offer new perspectives and ideas, sparking conversations that deepen your connection. Seasonal reflections are another powerful tool. As seasons change, take time to reflect on your growth. Evaluate what's working and what isn't, and set new intentions. It's like a spiritual spring cleaning, clearing the clutter and making room for the latest. These practices aren't just exercises; they're commitments to ongoing development. They're opportunities to learn, grow, and strengthen your relationship. So, as you move forward, embrace each new season with open arms and an open heart, ready to explore the richness and depth that ongoing growth brings.

## 10.4 LEGACY OF LOVE: BUILDING A RELATIONSHIP THAT INSPIRES OTHERS

Think about that couple you know who seem to have it all figured out. They're not perfect, but their love and faith radiate, creating a ripple effect that touches everyone around them. This is the essence of leaving a legacy of love. Building an inspiring relationship makes you a beacon of hope and faith for future generations. Your commitment to a Christ-centered marriage can serve as a role model, showing others that love, rooted in faith, is not only possible but profoundly fulfilling. Encouraging others to pursue similar marriages means inspiring those around you to strive for relationships that reflect Christ's love and grace. Your journey becomes a testament to the power of faith in transforming lives, demonstrating that a relationship centered on Christ can withstand the test of time.

Creating a legacy of love involves actively engaging with your community. Share your testimonies and experiences, letting others see how faith has shaped and sustained your relationship. These stories can offer encouragement and guidance, serving as a roadmap for those navigating their relational paths. Consider taking on mentorship or leadership roles within your faith community. By guiding younger couples or those struggling with their relationships, you pass on the wisdom and insights you've gained. This involvement strengthens your bond and enriches your community, fostering a culture of support and growth. As you invest in others, you'll find that your relationship blossoms, enriched by the connections and shared experiences that mentorship and leadership bring.

An inspiring relationship has the power to influence others in remarkable ways. It encourages positive change and growth for you and those around you. Your actions and words can inspire others to strive for deeper connections, fostering a community that values love, faith, and mutual support. Through shared experiences, you strengthen community bonds, creating a network of relationships that uplift and inspire. These connections act as a safety net, supporting and encouraging during challenging times. As your legacy grows, it becomes a living testament to the transformative power of love, inspiring others to reach the same heights in their relationships. The impact of your legacy of love extends beyond your immediate circle, touching lives in ways you may never fully realize.

To promote an inspiring relationship, consider engaging in legacy-building activities. Writing a family mission statement based on shared values is a powerful way to articulate your vision and goals. This statement is a guiding star, reminding you of the principles that ground your relationship. Hosting events celebrating and reflecting on your relationship's journey offers another avenue for sharing your legacy. Gather friends and family to celebrate milestones, share stories, and reflect on the growth you've experienced together. These events honor your journey and inspire and encourage others, demonstrating the joy and fulfillment that a Christ-centered relationship brings.

## 10.5 A UNIFIED FRONT: FACING CHALLENGES TOGETHER

Picture two people in a canoe, paddling on a serene lake. Now imagine if they paddled in opposite directions—chaos, right? Relationships thrive on unity, especially when facing life's inevitable challenges. Presenting a united front isn't about being identical in thoughts and actions; it's about collaboration. When challenges arise, whether it's a financial hiccup or a difference in parenting styles, working together to address and overcome obstacles strengthens your bond. Unity means supporting each other unequivocally during adversity, like a sturdy bridge over turbulent waters. It's about having each other's back and reassuring that you're in this together no matter what.

Maintaining unity is an ongoing effort, like tending a fire to keep it burning bright. Effective communication and problem-solving skills are the kindling and logs that fuel this fire. Develop a habit of discussing challenges openly and seeking solutions rather than blaming each other. Regular check-ins can help you stay aligned, ensuring you're both on the same page. Encouraging mutual support and understanding is vital, too. Acknowledge each other's strengths and work together to fill in the gaps. This mutual support fosters a cohesive marriage, creating a safe space where both of you feel valued and understood. It's like forming a human chain in a game of tug-of-war, where each spouse's strength complements and amplifies the other's.

Facing challenges together enhances resilience and growth. When you tackle obstacles side by side, you build trust and confidence in your marriage. Each resolved challenge becomes a brick in the foundation of your relationship, adding stability and strength. This shared resilience makes future challenges less daunting, knowing that you've weathered storms before and can do so again. The trust gained from overcoming difficulties creates a deep and unwavering bond, much like a well-tended garden that flourishes despite occasional droughts. This process strengthens your relationship and enriches your growth as you learn from each other and the challenges you face.

Consider activities that promote teamwork and unity. Creating a joint action plan for addressing specific challenges can be incredibly effective. Sit together, list the issues, brainstorm solutions, and assign tasks. It's like plotting a course on a treasure map, where each step brings you closer to resolution. Engaging in team-building exercises can also reinforce your connection. These could be as simple as tackling a DIY project at home or more adventurous, like taking a class together. These activities encourage collaboration and highlight the importance of working together towards a common goal. They remind us that, while the challenges may be daunting, the strength of your marriage is more than capable of overcoming them.

## 10.6 EMBRACING GRACE: A RELATIONSHIP ROOTED IN FORGIVENESS AND LOVE

Imagine grace as a soft light that fills every corner of your relationship, casting away shadows of resentment and misunderstanding. Embracing grace fosters compassion and understanding in every interaction, like a gentle breeze that soothes and calms. It encourages you to see beyond the surface to the heart of your spouse's intentions and struggles. Prioritizing forgiveness becomes the cornerstone of your relationship, where acknowledging mistakes paves the way for healing and growth. This approach doesn't just mend what's broken; it strengthens the bond, creating a marriage that thrives on love and acceptance. By viewing each other through a lens of grace, you nurture a resilient and tender relationship, capable of weathering storms and basking in the sunshine.

Cultivating a grace-filled relationship requires intentional effort, but the rewards are profound. Begin by practicing empathy and active listening during conflicts. It's about stepping into your spouse's shoes, feeling the pinch of their worries, and hearing the unspoken words behind their silence. This practice transforms conflict from a battlefield into a space for connection and understanding. Establishing rituals of forgiveness and reconciliation can also weave grace into the fabric of your relationship. Whether it's a weekly check-in to clear the air or a simple gesture of acknowledgment, these rituals create a rhythm of forgiveness that becomes second nature. They remind you that love is not about perfection but choosing each other, flaws and all, every day.

The impact of grace on relationship dynamics is transformative. It reduces resentment like a balm on a wound, promoting healing and paving the way for deeper intimacy. Grace builds a foundation of trust and mutual respect, where both spouses feel safe to express their true selves without fear of judgment. This foundation becomes a launchpad for growth, allowing you to explore new depths of connection and understanding. As grace permeates your interactions, it transforms your relationship into a sanctuary of love and acceptance. It fosters an environment where both spouses can thrive, supported by the unwavering belief in each other's goodness and potential.

Consider activities that emphasize forgiveness and love. Engage in regular reflection on personal growth in grace. This practice allows you to track your progress, acknowledge areas of improvement, and celebrate victories. Creating a gratitude and forgiveness journal can also be a powerful tool. Use it to document moments of grace, both given and received and express gratitude for the love and understanding that define your relationship. This journal becomes a testament to your journey, a written record of the grace that sustains and enriches your marriage. As you embrace grace, remember that it is not a destination but a continuous process of learning and love, a path that leads to a deeper, more fulfilling relationship.

## Want to Help Other Couples?

As your own love and strength as a couple deepen, it's natural that you'd want to help other couples strengthen their bond through their faith in God. Here's an easy way for you to do that right now.

Simply by sharing your honest opinion of this book and a little about your own experience, you'll give new readers hope and show them a way to use their faith to guide them.

# WANT TO HELP OTHERS?

Thank you so much for your support. Here's to a lifetime of love and unity.

>>> **Click here to leave your review on Amazon.**

# CONCLUSION

Wow, what a journey we've been on together! As we wrap up this devotional, let's take a moment to reflect on the path we've traveled. We've explored how to build a strong, Christ-centered relationship filled with faith, love, and a sprinkle of humor. Think of it as a road trip where you've packed your bags with all the essential tools and insights (and maybe a few snacks) to keep your marriage thriving.

Throughout this book, we've touched on some big themes. We've looked at God's plan for marriage, drawing lessons from Adam and Eve. We've explored the roles and responsibilities that come with being in a marriage, and we've dived into the power of faith as the bedrock of your relationship. We even tackled conflict resolution and celebrated the beautiful chaos of intimacy. Each chapter has been crafted to offer practical guidance and spiritual wisdom, helping you navigate the ups and downs of married life.

So, what are the major takeaways? First, embracing roles and responsibilities will give the husband-and-wife goals to work on and grow. Employing godly communication is key. Speaking each other's love language and active listening can transform misunderstandings into meaningful conversations. Embrace faith as your guiding star, and don't shy away from difficult discussions. These moments are opportunities for growth and connection. Also, remember that emotional, spiritual, and physical intimacy is the glue that holds everything together. And, of course, never underestimate the power of humor to lighten the mood and deepen your bond.

Now, here's where it gets exciting. It's time to put all this into action. I encourage you to take the principles and exercises we've discussed and make them a living part of your relationship. Carve out time for devotionals, commit to regular date nights, and don't forget to celebrate even the most minor victories together. Remember, transformation doesn't happen overnight. It requires dedication, effort, and a willingness to grow together. Start by setting a few goals, maybe even craft a mission statement for your relationship. Whatever you do, do it with love and intention.

Let's not forget the vision that has guided this book. It's about nurturing a relationship that mirrors Christ's love—selfless, forgiving, and enduring. See your marriage as a journey of faith, love, and continual growth. Let this vision inspire you to walk hand in hand, finding joy in the shared experiences and challenges that life throws your way.

As we conclude, I want to express my heartfelt gratitude. Thank you for inviting me, Rev. Fred Reese, into your journey. Your commitment to strengthening your marriage through faith is truly inspiring. Remember, you're not alone on this path. I'm cheering you on, and so is a community of believers who understand the joy and fulfillment a Christ-centered relationship brings.

And finally, as you move forward, I offer you a blessing. May your love grow deeper with each passing day. May your faith remain steadfast, guiding you through every storm and sunshine. May you always find unity and joy in each other, celebrating your marriage's beautiful dance.

Here's to a future filled with love, laughter, and endless blessings. Keep your hearts open, your spirits high, and your eyes on the path God has set before you. You've got this!

# REFERENCES

*Lessons from the First Marriage* | https://www.walkintruth.net/chapters-8-12/lessons-from-the-first-marriage.html

*Selfless Marriage: Ephesians 5:21–33* https://www.cbeinternational.org/resource/selfless-marriage-ephesians-521-33/

*15 Faithful Ways Christian Couples Can Strengthen Their ...* https://churchandmentalhealth.com/15-faithful-ways-christian-couples-can-strengthen-their-relationship/

*Marriage: A Covenant, Not a Contract* https://ftc.co/resource-library/blog-entries/marriage-a-covenant-not-a-contract/

*What are The 5 Love Languages?* https://5lovelanguages.com/learn

*Using Active Listening to Enhance Your Relationships* https://extension.usu.edu/relationships/faq/using-active-listening-to-enhance-your-relationships

*10 Expert-Backed Communication Strategies for Stronger ...* https://www.deltapsychology.com/psychology-ponderings/10-expert-backed-communication-strategies-for-stronger-relationships

*How Forgiveness Can Transform Your Marriage* https://www.gottman.com/blog/forgiveness-can-transform-marriage/

*The Role of Spirituality in Couples Therapy* https://www.abundancetherapycenter.com/blog/the-role-of-spirituality-in-couples-therapy

*Building Intimacy through Couple Prayer* https://dcfi.org/resources/articles/building-intimacy-through-couple-prayer/

*Statistics on the Impact of Marriage Devotionals on ...* https://newbookrecommendation.com/statistics-on-the-impact-of-marriage-devotionals-on-relationships/

*Living Your Faith: 7 Ways to Integrate Christian Values into ...* https://christiancounselingco.com/living-your-faith/

*Christian Conflict Resolution in Marriage: 7 Biblical Ways* https://marriagerescue.org/christian-conflict-resolution-in-marriage-7-biblical-ways/

*Marital Conflict, Depressive Symptoms, and Functional ...* https://pmc.ncbi.nlm.nih.gov/articles/PMC2507765/

*Christian Marriage Counseling: Definition, Techniques, \u0026 ...* https://www.verywellmind.com/christian-marriage-counseling-definition-techniques-and-efficacy-5219586

*What is the Importance of Forgiveness for Christians?* https://clothedwithdignityco.com/importance-of-forgiveness-christian/

*The Importance of Vulnerability in Healthy Relationships* https://www.psychologyto

day.com/us/blog/happy-healthy-relationships/202203/the-importance-of-vulnera
bility-in-healthy-relationships

*Spiritual Intimacy: What It Is & How to Build It In Relationships* https://www.choos
ingtherapy.com/spiritual-intimacy/

*109 Fun Date Night Ideas to Inspire Romance* https://www.theknot.com/content/
date-ideas

*Giving Thanks: How Gratitude Strengthens Relationships* https://www.psychologyto
day.com/us/blog/evidence-based-living/202311/giving-thanks-how-gratitude-
strengthens-relationships

*Krista Williams On What To Do If Your Spouse Isn't Spiritual* https://almost30.com/
blog/2021/11/11/krista-williams-spirituality-and-relationships/

*How Mental Health & Spirituality in Relationships Can ...* https://www.marriage.
com/advice/relationship/spirituality-role-in-relationship/

*How To Balance Spiritual Life And Family Expectations?* https://medium.com/bupub
lication/how-to-balance-spiritual-life-and-family-expectations-5c30a53f8d41

*Interfaith Marriage Advice: Navigating Different Faith Traditions* https://wezoree.
com/inspiration/interfaith-marriage-advice-navigating-different-faith-traditions/

*A time-tested routine for spiritual formation - Growing Faith* https://growingfaith.
com.au/articles/a-time-tested-routine-for-spiritual-formation

*Choosing a Marriage Accountability Spouse* https://buildyourmarriage.org/choosing-
marriage-accountability-spouse/

*The Power of Journaling for Couples: Building A Better ...* https://www.rosebud.app/
blog/journaling-for-couples

*Celebrating Milestones in Marriages: A Joyful Journey of Love ...* https://www.
bbcatholic.org.au/hornsby/news-events/blogs/celebrating-milestones-in-
marriages-a-joyful-journey-of-love-and-commitment

*How Constantly Staying Busy Affects Our Well-Being* https://www.verywellmind.
com/how-the-glorification-of-busyness-impacts-our-well-being-4175360

*Spiritual Practices and Devotional Resources for Couples* https://www.umcdisciple
ship.org/resources/spiritual-practices-and-devotional-resources-for-couples

*Applying the Bible to Modern Life | AGW MINISTRIES* https://applygodsword.com/
applying-the-bible-to-modern-life/

*Managing Life Transitions Together: A Guide for Couples* https://www.selfspaceseat
tle.com/blog/2024/2/25/managing-life-transitions-together-a-guide-for-couples

*How Small Groups Build Your Marriage* https://buildyourmarriage.org/how-small-
groups-build-your-marriage/

*What Christian Mentoring Is and How to Do It* https://www.cru.org/us/en/train-and-
grow/help-others-grow/mentoring.html

*11 Compelling Benefits of Volunteering as Couples* https://www.marriage.com/
advice/relationship/benefits-of-volunteering/

*Weekend to Remember Marriage Retreat* https://www.familylife.com/weekend-to-remember/

*6 Responsibilities God Gave Adam and Eve in Eden* https://www.heroesbibletrivia.org/en/adam-and-eve-eden-responsibilities/

*A Simple Guide to Setting Faith-Based Goals* https://jazminnfrank.com/a-simple-guide-to-setting-faith-based-goals/

*Christian Community: The Secret Ingredient for a Stronger ...* https://www.christianity.com/wiki/marriage/christian-community-the-secret-ingredient-for-a-stronger-marriage.html

*Giving Thanks: How Gratitude Strengthens Relationships* https://www.psychologytoday.com/us/blog/evidence-based-living/202311/giving-thanks-how-gratitude-strengthens-relationships

*30+ Powerful Marriage Quotes That Will Inspire Every Couple.MARRIAGE AFTER GOD. 19 December 2022. Accessed January 17, 2025.* https://marriageaftergod.com/30-favorite-marriage-quotes-bible-verses/.

Made in United States
Troutdale, OR
05/04/2025

31095359R10076